T0067287

The ROAD *to* Reynolds

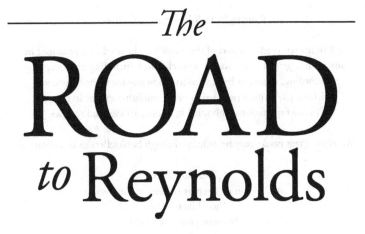

BRYAN L. CARSON

WESTBOW°
PRESS
A DIVISION OF THOMAS NELSON
& ZONDERVAN

WestBow Press books may be ordered through booksellers or by contacting:

WestBow Press
A Division of Thomas Nelson & Zondervan
1663 Liberty Drive
Bloomington, IN 47403
www.westbowpress.com
1 (866) 928-1240

ISBN: 978-1-4908-7332-9 (sc)
ISBN: 978-1-4908-7331-2 (e)

Library of Congress Control Number: 2015904583

Print information available on the last page.

WestBow Press rev. date: 05/28/2015

Chapter 1

As I sit here on this porch in the hot afternoon sun, I can't tell you how grateful I am to be here with Mister Carson and his third son Joseph. This family was torn apart by the War Between the States and is just now beginning to heal from the wounds of that war more than ten years later. If it weren't for the war, we could've been sitting out here, enjoying this beautiful sunset with Mister Carson's 3 other sons as well. But you took 'em Lawd, you took 'em…..Let's see where this all started.

Saturday June 15th of '1839 is a day I'll never forget, Lawd will I never forget that beautiful day down by the banks of the muddy Flint River. Mister Carson's two oldest boys John Thomas and James Alston set out to go swimming in the river with their mule Bess. Well, when they were through swimming, they tried and tried and tried to get Bess to go swimming as well. Well,

1

knowing boys will be boys, when that mule refused to go anywhere near that water, John and James figured maybe the easiest way to get Bess into the water would be to light her tail on fire. Lawd have mercy did it ever work. That beast dove into that muddy water like a catfish being thrown back in. As I came upon the riverbank and witnessed the very end of their mischief, I scolded John Thomas. "John Thomas, ain't you got a lick of sense in that thick skull of yours? You know your daddy's gonna tear your backside out when he finds out about what you and Mister James done did to Bess! Now get her up out of that river and take your brother home. Go on git." "Yes, George. We're sorry for lighting Bess' tail on fire," replied James and John Thomas in unison. "Well you oughtta be. How'd you like it if she did that to you?" "I reckon that'd hurt real bad," John Thomas replied. "You know you ain't posed to be no bad influence on your little brother James. He's only 6 years old, and here you is almost 14, almost a man, and you trying to teach him it's all right to light Mister Carson's farm animals on fire?

Lawd have mercy, y'all better get home before I do!" "Yes, George." When we got home Mister Carson made John Thomas go get a switch for both him and his little brother James. When John Thomas came back the first time with switches, Mister Carson said, "Boy, if you bring me a twig like that again, I'll go get the switch, and y'all won't like the one I pick!" I reckon those rascals had trouble sitting down awhile after that, but they never did that to Bess, or any other livestock owned by Mister Carson again. After supper, the boys went to their rooms while Mizz Carson nursed their brand new baby brother Joseph Perryman Carson, born two weeks before. Lawd have mercy, you never saw such a smile on Mister Carson, or on his wife Mizz Martha Goodwin Raines Carson after Mister Joseph was born at the Carson home. John Thomas was their first child, while James was the fourth, and Joseph was their seventh baby. 'Course they had sisters, but they had nurses for 'em. My job was to look after the Carson boys, & reckon I quite enjoyed their company, 'cept 'course when they were lighting mule tails on fire.

Joseph Jefferson Carson was born on April 16th, 1802, and was wed to Martha Goodwin Raines Carson on October 29th, 1823 in Jones County, Georgia. They happened to get married on Mizz Martha's 15th birthday. Little did the young happy couple know what life would have in store for 'em. When I got home that night, my wife Lula was in a tizzy the likes of which I never saw before. "George, why you let dem boys light Bess on fiah like 'dat? You know dey don't know no better den dat?" "Well, Honey, by the time I got there, they had just about done it, and there was nothing I could do to stop 'em." "Ugh huh, you shoulda ben dere making sho dey doan git in no trouble. They upset Mister Carson something fierce, and he almost get old Mizz Martha upset, but I tell her, doan worry Mizz Martha, I make sho my George he do a better job of watching dem boys next time." And she tell me, "Don't fret over it Lula. I know he will." Den she jess sat dere all googly eyed over dat new baby of hers.

So doan you upset dem again George Carson 'cause you ain't doing what you posed to be doing! You heah me?" "Yessum. I won't let 'em act up like that again 'cause Mista and Mizz Carson, they've been real good to us, and I wouldn't want to let 'em down again iffin I can hep it. If it weren't for Mister Carson we wouldn't have this nice little cottage in the back of their property, and all this food we're so blessed to have from 'em." "Dat's right George, and doan you forget it. Now get cleaned up fo supper, it almost ready." "Yessum."

When I think about my wife, I think that if I had to look for a wife all over again, I'd pick her every single time! She really is good to me and our 5 children. Though, you don't wanna catch her when she's in a bilious humor. Her mood can go from kind and loving to dragon slayer faster than a frog can catch a skeeter with his tongue. When did I first meet Lula? I reckon it was in the spring of '25. She was a beautiful young thing, just 16 years old and personal servant to Mizz Martha. Lawd does Lula love Mizz Martha! Can't nobody get within 5 feet of Mizz Martha without incurring the wrath of Lula, 'cept 'course it's Mister Carson. Lula has given me 5 beautiful children that are the apple of my eye. Lawd what a woman! On fire one minute, then ice cold the next.

After I cleaned up, I went in for supper and once again I was ready to dig into my feast once I said grace. We all joined hands then I prayed to the good Lawd. "Dear Lawd, thank you so much for this feast for which we're most thankful to you for your generosity. Thank you for all your many blessings, and bless this food to the nourishment of our bodies. In Jesus' great name we pray. Amen." "This looks mighty fine Momma. You sho are too good to us." "Mmmmm hmmm. Next time you let dem rascals light Bess tail on fiah, it goan be you who get dey tail on fiah too!"

After we cleaned the table, and got the children ready for bed, we said our prayers before bed. "Thank you dear Lawd for another day of your blessed providence. Help us to get a good night sleep, and to glorify thy great name Lawd Jesus. In thy name we pray. Amen."

"Good night chillun, you gotta get a good night's sleep for school tomorrow. We slept a good night sleep, and got up way before sunrise like we always did. Lula was already over at Carson House helping with breakfast, while I was left to get our youngins up and get them fed before school. They don't yet realize what a privilege it is to learn how to read and write. I guess I learned how to read and write from going to church with the Carson's. Reading the Bible and the hymnals that is, taught me how to read and write when I was already a grown man. Now my children get to go to school in the mornings, but in the afternoon is when they set about to do their chores. At night before they go to bed I'll read to them a little bit, and they'll read some too, to practice. We read from the Bible, newspapers, & Harpers Weekly. Mostly we read anything we can get our hands on. Lula, poor thing can't read or write at all. But, me and the kids are trying to teach her when we can get her to slow down a bit. She gets so frustrated when she tries to pronounce something and can't do it that sometimes she'll go into a lathering tirade that a body would do well to steer clear of. I sure do hope Lula learns how to read one day, 'cause if I heard the preacher say it once, I've heard him say it a thousand times, "Beloved, in lots of learning there is great power." Lawd, how that man can preach. Don't get me wrong, sometimes at the end of church he'll suddenly get excited and preach for another 20 minutes and my stomach's so weak I feel like I'm a gonna faint, even though we all had a big ham and egg breakfast. As a matter of fact, one time he come visiting the Carsons for dinner after church, and he kept going on and on in his blessing so that it perturbed those Carson boys so bad, that after dinner they went out and put a spur underneath the preacher's saddle. Lawd, you shoulda seen old Reverend Glover when he got on his horse and that horsetook off right underneath him, leaving him hanging in midair before he fell on his head! Now I can't prove to you that those boys put a spur underneath his saddle, but me and Mister Carson exchanged a knowing look right after it happened, and since he didn't like having to wait 15 minutes to eat either because of the

Preacher man's long blessing, he never said nothing to the boys about it.

Although I did hear him tell John Thomas one day afterwards that when he was growing up in S.C., there was a boy who put a spur underneath his neighbors saddle, and when the neighbor found out who did it, he shot him. Mister Carson told me later that he thought John Thomas' face turned redder than an apple. 'Cept Mister Carson also told me that he made that story up. After getting the children to the schoolhouse, I went over to the Carson House. It was after breakfast, and all the field hands were already out in the field, and Mister Carson was on the porch, so I bid him good morning, as he said "Good morning George. Looks like it might rain today." "Yes, suh," I said. "Have a seat George." "Yes, suh." "George, you reckon John Thomas or James'll be able to sit comfortably in a wooden chair for a while?" He chuckled and so did I, and I said, "No suh, I reckon not." We sat and enjoyed the view of the fields and all that Georgia cotton being picked. Lawd what a mess that was. I sure was glad I worked inside the house, instead of outside. Leastways some of them field hands ate better than me. Mister Carson takes good care of 'em, and he's good to their families too. If any of his servants need to see the doctor or want to go to his church he's more than obliged to take care of 'em. But even though they ate better than I did, they can have that job. Growing up as a kid, every summer would find me out there in them fields picking that white Georgia cotton, and Lawd was that stuff sticky, and that's not even taking into count if you got thorns in your hand. "Last night after supper I went in to talk to the boys after I'd whipped 'em, and I asked 'em what they learned from their foolishness, and James said he learned that Bess don't like to have her tail lit on fire, and John Thomas said he learned that he doesn't like to disappoint you George. You take good care of those boys, and they enjoy going fishing with you, and hunting deer and turkeys. I reckon what I'm trying to say is that whether you realize it or not George, you mean the world to those boys, and I just thought you ought to know." I was thunderstuck! 'Course I had been around 'em everyday of their whole lives, & I was just doing my job to look after 'em. I had no idea they looked up to me like an older brother, or an uncle, and I didn't know what to say. "Thank you, Mister Carson.

Them is good boys, but every now and then they get an idea to do something, and next thing you know something's broke, or been blown up. But they're fine young men, and I'm looking forward to teaching Mister Joseph how to hunt and fish one day too." Mister Carson smiled and nodded, taking another puff on his pipe. He bought his pipe tobacco from Virginia, and it was called Virginia Cavendish. Sometimes on a Saturday night we sit here on his porch and smoke our pipes. Lawd, they make some fine tobacco up in Virginia. One time I asked him, "Mister Carson, how come the tobacco they make up in Ole Virginia is so much better than our Georgia tobacco?" "Well George, I reckon I don't rightly know. However, a man from Virginia once told me it's because the soil up there is sandier than ours here in middle Georgia." "Well Suh, I hope we can always get our tobacco from up there in Ole Virginia." "I do as well, George." After school that day I took the boys hunting to see if we could find us a deer. We have a spot in the woods where we can normally find a deer or two, and today was no different. As we sat up on the small hill we were able to see 3 deer walk right in front of us. John Thomas was a good shot by now, and James was just now learning to shoot pretty good. "John Thomas, you get the one on the far left over yonder. James will get the one on the far right." "Yes George," they both replied. John Thomas sat down on one knee and aimed in on the left, while James lay flat on his belly and looked down the barrel of his rifle and took aim at his deer while his brother did the same. After 10 seconds I said, "Okay boys. Y'all ready to shoot?" "Yes," came the whisper from both of 'em. "Okay, I'm gonna count to 3, and when I get to three I want each of you to shoot at your deer okay?" "Yes George," came their whispered reply. "All right, 1......2".........just then John Thomas let out the loudest sneeze I ever heard! It was so loud he could've raised the dead in Erebus for all you knew. Next thing I knew, the deer on the left made a right and went back into the woods and John Thomas stood up and tracked the deer through the end of his rifle watching it run about a quarter of a mile before he hit the woods.

John Thomas calmly aimed at the upper chest of the deer on the end of his rifle, and after calmly taking a gentle breath, he let go of his breath, gently applied pressure to the trigger, and was slightly shocked when the rifle went off. Meanwhile, the round hit the deer in his right back leg, but after a second, the deer was nowhere to be found. The doe which had been in the middle of the pack smartly escaped when it noticed it wasn't being targeted, and fled safely through the woods. When the report of John Thomas' rifle went off, the deer James was aiming in on got spooked, and not knowing which way to run, ran straight at James and me. He must've been a ten point buck and weighed over 200 lbs. easy, and here he was coming straight at us. At 150 yards away he's gonna be on us in no time if James don't take the shot NOW! 100 yards, 80… "James SHOOT HIM!" 50, 25, 10 yards between us, and James is frightened, staring bug eyed at the 200 lb. behemoth about to crush us when another report of a rifle rang out in the air, and there stood John Thomas still aiming in on the deer until it went down, and then he set his rifle down. Lawd, I reckon as soon as James saw that his enemy was dead he burst into a squall that coulda raised the heavens! "James, James, it's gonna be all right. You just got scared is all. It happens to everybody." "Ikno.. kno….know George. When he was just standing there I was fine, but when he came running straight at me I didn't know what to do and got scared." "I know, I know. But, when a scary animal is coming straight at you, there is only one thing you have to do, and it's relax, aim straight at him, and gently pull the trigger. If you don't do it EXACTLY THAT, it's gonna be him that ate you, and not the other way around.'"Nice shooting

John Thomas! You just kept James and me from having railroad tracks all over us. Come on, let's go get the first one you got." "Thanks, George!" All three of us got up and went into the woods to find John Thomas' deer. "Look George, there's her blood!" "Yes suh, sho nuff is. Okay boys, be on the lookout 'cause she's hurt real bad right now, and when an animal is hurt they can be even more dangerous than if they was fine." We walked almost a mile 'til John Thomas saw her, sitting up on a bluff licking her wound. Her eyeballs were bulging out, and she was in a lot of pain. Even from a 100 yards away I could tell all that.

"John Thomas, aim straight for her head, and put her out of her misery." So, John Thomas spread his legs shoulder width apart, away from the deer, and he sighted his rifle in and gently squeezed the trigger. Boom! After this, the po thing was out of her misery. "John Thomas go get Bess and the wagon. We'll get her when you get back, and then we'll get the other one you got." "Yes George, I'll be right back."

When John Thomas got back we loaded the Doe into the wagon, and then we went over and got the other one that just about ran over James and me. Deer ain't real smart, anything that would run straight at someone whose aiming a loaded gun at 'em needs to have their head examined. When we got home, Mister Carson met us out back of the house. "Afternoon, Suh."

"Good afternoon gentlemen, what have we got here?" "Father, we shot two deer. This one's a Doe, while this one here is a 10 pointer!" "Indeed it is. Good hunting boys, now go get ready for supper." "Yes, Suh," they both replied and hurried off to wash up for another of Lula's delicious fried chicken suppers Lawd, could that woman cook up some amazing delicacies! What would we all do without her? "How'd the hunt go, George?" "I reckon it went good, Suh. We saw three deer, and I told John Thomas to get the one on the left, and James to get the one on the right. Well, right when I was telling 'em to shoot, John Thomas lets out a cannonball of a sneeze and it spooked the deer like the devil, and they tucked tail and took off. All'cept that biggun, and he ran straight at James & me. Well Mister James froze up, and before he was upon us John Thomas shot him! Woo wee Mister Carson, I thought Mister James and I were about to be mincemeat." "Yes suh, you sure were lucky George! Lucky for y'all I taught John Thomas how to shoot so well." "Yes suh, that boy could hit a silver dollar at 100 yards." "Okay George, can you take the wagon to the barn and get Big John and Jeremiah to dress these deer for us?" "'Course I can, Mister Carson." "Thank you, George."

I nodded my head with pride and headed to back of the house where the barn was. When I got there Big John said, "Hey dere George, what ya got in 'dat wagon?" "I got us two deer here. Mister John, and Mister James & me got us a big buck, and a skinny doe." "Ain't no meat on dat skinny one, but 'dat biggun, reckon he could feed the Carson's and all of us fo a week straight, Sunday to Sunday" Jeremiah said. "Come on, Jeremiah, we got a lot of work to do befo we eat any this fine venison George done brought us. Thank you, Mista George." "Thank y'all for dressing 'em for us." With all that done, I headed home to check on my family and eat some of Lula's delicious fried chicken. When I sat down at the supper table I looked on with pride at Lula's creation. Before us all was a platter of hot fried chicken, mashed potatoes, corn on the cob, peas, collard greens, fried okra, black eyed peas, & corn bread. Oh dear Lawd if that woman made Pe-can pie, take me now Lawd!!! I said a quick blessing 'cause, not that I was starving, but absolutely couldn't wait any longer to dig into this feast.

We had it good on the Carson Plantation, we were never hungry, quite the contrary. Some nights like tonight I had to let my belt out a few notches so my stomach could breathe better. Sitting out on the porch of my house that night with Lula we talked about how blessed we were. "George, was 'dat deer really coming straight fo you and Mista James?" "Yesum." "I'm so glad Mista John Thomas shot him 'den!" "Me too, Momma! Me too."

Well the years went by and Mizz Carson had more children, and so did Lula, but that was fine. We all had plenty of room and plenty of food to eat. It was about 1854 by then I reckon, and Mister Carson bought a plantation from the Wilbur family who moved back up North because of the rising tensions between North and South. By then my children had grown up and been married for a while now. My oldest had 3 children of his own, and Lula and I had 12 grandbabies. We were so proud, and you shoulda seen the look on Lula's face every time she held one of her grandbabies, she would just smile at 'em, and make funny faces, and they would laugh, and laugh. Lawd, would they laugh!

Two of Mister Carson's sons, John Thomas and James were all grown up by now, and the last two Joseph and Robert were getting there as well. The youngest, Mister

Robert Hall Carson came into this world on Thursday April 2nd, 1846. Baby boy Robert was definitely a surprise to the Carson's but what a bundle of joy that little baby was to 'em! Lawd have mercy! All in all, I'd say life was as fine it'd ever been around here in Macon County, Georgia. Yes suh, the good Lawd had blessed us in every aspect of our lives. Mister Carson gave me 25 acres of my own to farm and raise crops on, and Lula & I had our own house on his property, that while not as big as his house, we paid no mind to it, for we thought it was the finest house you ever saw. There was never a shortage on the farm of meat or vegetables, summer & fall the harvest was so great that Mister Carson always had plenty extra to give to the folks in our community who were less fortunate than us, and for this they were always grateful. Mister Carson always said he didn't mind and was glad to do it. Seems like it was last year that Dr. Coleman founded the town of Reynolds about 5 miles northwest of us, county of Taylor. Reynolds was an exciting place to go to in those days, just getting started up in the middle of nowhere like that and all, and next thing you know there's a brand new town right in the middle of Taylor County. Reckon one day there's gonna be a whole lot of folks living in Reynolds, and that's good 'cause it don't take no time for us to get to it if we need to go to market. Now Atlanta, Georgia, woo wee, Reynolds don't hold a candle to Atlanta! Last year Mister Carson brought me up there, and that town is enormous! We stayed up there two days while he was on business, and while he was doing his business I would just walk up and down Peachtree Street and look at all the fine wares those merchants and shopkeepers had in their windows. Why, one man I met told me he was gonna open up a store and sell clothes for ladies from Paris, France! I can't never remember his name, Mr. Rich? It was something like that, I can't ever remember 'cause my memory's not as good as it used to be, but I do remember the important things in life. Though it ain't hard to forget how fast Mister Carson's boys have grown up by now. Let's see John Thomas is 30 years old now, and 7 years ago he married Mizz Susan Saphronia Howe Carson.

Then James married Mizz Melissa Bryan Carson about 6 months ago. Before you know it Joseph and Robert will be up and married, then Mister and Mizz Carson won't have any more sons to marry off.

Around 1859, Mister Carson purchased a big plantation from Mister Hiram B. Hicks with around

2000 acres backing up to the west bank of the Flint River. The new Carson House was just grand, and everybody loved it. The front of the property was right off of River Road in Northern Macon County, Georgia. The Carson's youngest boy Robert absolutely loved the new place. He and I'd spend hours hunting in those woods, or fishing in that muddy Flint River, and we both had a grand time! One night after supper, Mister Carson and I were rocking in our chairs on his front porch enjoying the grand sunset. "George, the good Lord's been real good to us, but I fear that time might be about to come to an end." "Why would that be Mister Carson? We got plenty to eat, roofs over our heads. The good Lawd has blessed us with fine health." Mister Carson didn't say anything, but laid his head back against his rocker and slowly puffed his pipe. Smoke lazily drifted upward toward the ceiling of the porch, and so I did the same thing. A long time went by and then Mister Carson sighed, and pulled his pipe out of his mouth. "George," he pointed with his pipe from left to right at the beautiful land he'd cultivated, and made very productive, "soon all this could be taken from us. We're about to go to war with the North, and if we lose they could take it all to make us pay for the war." "Surely the Yankees wouldn't take the house, and the land you gave me would they Mister Carson?" "I'm afraid they would George." "Why Suh, I ain't ever even done nothing to bother no Yankee. How can they come take my land, and my house that you gave me?" "George, I'm so sorry, but I'm afraid it ain't quite that simple. You see since I gave you that house, and that land, they may think you're complicit in the fight against the North, and take it as spoils of war. I hear that those folks up there do things differently than we do down here.

Why I hear they don't even let black folks worship with 'em in their own churches up there. If that ain't a sin, Lord have mercy, I don't know what one is. I fervently hope and pray that the gentleman who told me that was wrong, and they do in fact let black men & women worship with 'em in their houses of worship up North. "Well why do they want to go to war with us over slavery when they won't even let black people in their own churches? That don't make any sense at all!" "No, it doesn't, George. That's what I heard someone say the other day at the market, heaven knows if it's true. "Anyway, I'm real concerned about my boys, George. I see the look in their eyes when they talk about going to war, and all the heroic actions they're going to take to kill the evil Yankee soldiers up there George. They don't know the first thing about war. First of all it's real lonely, for you're away from your family for months or even years at a time, and living in wretched conditions, which compared to how they live now would mean they live like kings here at home. Fighting in those hot wool uniforms, burning up in summer, and freezing cold in the winter. You reckon that would be a glorious experience, George? I think not, and let's not forget, let's not forget that in the midst of ALL THIS, somebody is out there trying to KILL YOU all the time! Why can't those folks up Washington just leave us alone? Have we done anything to 'em? Dear Lord, please protect our nation from being thrown into a chaotic war of North versus South. Amen. Good night, George." "Good night, Suh." I walked the little way back to our house and sat out on the porch and tried not to think of a war, but I couldn't help it. Mister Carson had good reason to be worried, for I have heard recently all 4 of his sons talking about joining the army of the Confederate States of America, if there is a war. Robert was just 13 then, and even HE was talking about going up North and killing Yankees. Good Lawd!

He's just knee high to a duck right now, & he wouldn't even be able to see a Yankee, much less kill him. Who does he reckon he is, King David versus Goliath? By now John Thomas, James, and Joseph were all fully grown men, and if there is going to be a war, they will all be in it. Mister Carson won't admit it, but it's true. Sad part is that John Thomas and James are married and have children. Will they leave their families and go up North to fight? They could all be killed, and then what would Mister Carson do? Can't they just stay here and fight if the Yankees bring their Army down here to fight? If they asked me to fight I reckon I would, but I'm probably getting a little long in the tooth for that.

Mister Carson had several dogs on his farm, and mostly he had retrievers. He's had a yellow female named Sadie for a while along with a brown male named King. Well, Sadie had pups a few years ago, and Mister Carson gave me the prettiest little black one of her litter, and I named him Jacob 'cause the Bible say's Jacob means "deceiver." Dear Lawd did he ever deceive us. That little pup was no bigger than the size of my hand when we got him, and today he's over a hundred pounds! Jake likes to go hunting and fishing with Robert and me, and when he's not doing that, or sleeping he likes to run around in the woods and hunt down raccoons. That dog is tough, 'cause raccoons are mean, but Jacob is the exact opposite of that. He loves to sit underneath the supper table and wait for scraps after supper. Sometimes he eats really well, and others he eats okay. I reckon it depends on whether Lula made fried chicken or meat loaf for supper. Let me put it to y'all like this, if we have fried chicken he eats all right. But, if we have meat loaf he eats like a king! But please don't tell Lula that, or I might have to sleep out there in the doghouse with him.

Chapter 2

1859 came and went, along with 1860. More rumors of war on the horizon, and when Abraham Lincoln was elected President on November 6, 1860 without a single southern vote, the dye was cast. With our nation on the brink of war, the mood around Carson House was intense. Every night after supper the men would retire to the library and discuss the current and latest rumors. Though Mister Carson didn't think Robert was old enough for these discussions, in light of the possibilities he allowed him because he realized Robert would probably one day have a hand in this game.

Mister Carson was nominated as a delegate to the state convention in Milledgeville, Georgia in the beginning of January 1961. When the vote for secession came to, he reluctantly voted for. Thus, with most of the states in the deep South voting to secede from the Union, they then began to prepare for a Northern invasion many thought would be ordered by Mister Lincoln. With almost all Southern states having seceded by now, we did however have a very quiet winter in 1861. That was all about to change in early spring of 1861, as Governor Francis W. Pickens of South Carolina was demanding the federal government to evacuate from Ft. Sumter Island, because it controls access to Charleston Harbor on all sides. On Wednesday December 26, 1860, U.S. Army Major Robert Anderson seized control of Fort Sumter, and was able to maintain control of the Island despite being outgunned and short on men, food, and weapons.

While Anderson raced all winter to get his big guns up and running, it wasn't meant to be, for on Friday April 12, 1861 at 4:30 in the morning Fort Sumter was barraged by artillery from all sides for 34 hours, until Major Anderson agreed to evacuate. Miraculously, there was no one killed on either side.

Back home everyone was happy that we had kicked the Yankees out of Charleston Harbor, but what nobody seemed to realize is that we had basically kicked a giant in the toe, and now he was mad. Two months after that on Monday June 15, 1861 John Thomas was commissioned as 1ˢᵗ Lt of Company C, 12ᵗʰ Georgia Regiment. After he enlisted, one day Mister Carson pulled me aside and said he wanted to talk to me. So went out onto his porch that night after supper, lit our pipes, and rocked in our chairs. The air was a little cooler than it normally was this time of year, but we didn't mind. In fact we were glad. It so hot down here in the summertime that you can take an egg and fry it in the pot underneath the sun without a fire, & tastes just the same as if you cooked it over the stove. Tomorrow would probably be hotter than hades anyway. And the gnats we have here, Lawd have mercy! In the summertime they're horrible! Smoke from my pipe helps run 'em off a little bit, but not always. At least in the winter time we don't have to worry about gnats so much.

"John Thomas enlisted in the Army of the Confederacy today, and he came to see me in his new uniform, wool and cotton dyed grey with Butternut. With that uniform on and the sword they gave him from Germany he looks like a true Southern gentleman. Susan's not too happy about it, though she tries to put up a stiff upper lip. George, we talked a few years ago about this coming war and the potential repercussions. George, you know John Thomas has always admired you the way you spent so much time with him growing up, and taking him hunting and fishing. Sometimes I thought he minded you better than me. George, this is hard of me to ask on account of Lula, but…" "what is it Suh?" "George, would you consider going with John Thomas when he goes off to War?

I know it would be a big sacrifice for you, and for Lula, but if you say yes we'll make sure that Lula's taken good care of and looked after in your absence." John Thomas and myself have always been real close, I've practically known him his whole life and always enjoyed his company, so what could I say to Mister Carson? "Suh, it would be an honor, and a privilege." "Thank you George! Thank you George! Miss Martha and I are so glad, and we know you'll take excellent care of him." "Yes, Suh, I will." "Okay, George, well I better head off to bed. We'll see ya in the morning. Good night." "Good night, Mister Carson." Lawd have mercy, looks like John Thomas and I are about to head off for war. Better go home and tell Lula, and pray for the best response I can get from her. "Dear Lawd, give me and John Thomas success in our war against the North. Almighty Lawd, ruler of the Universe, guide us and keep us, and may we forever turn to thou in our hour in need. In thy mighty and majestic name of Jesus I pray, Amen."

Lula weren't too happy when I gave her the news, but, and she shocked me a little bit, said she kinda expected it. "Lots of 'dem boys gonna need porters George, and I guruntee you de man of de house ain't gonna ax any other porters to go up there with their bosses and fight. Dey gone say, 'Hey, Big John, pack yo truck, youse gonna off to wuh with Mista William, or Mista Cletus, or whoever.' De point, George, is 'dat Mista Carson *axed you if you wanted to go.* Reckon you coulda said no, but least he axed you. George, Baby, I know you take good care of dat gentmen John Thomas, and I be here *in our house* when y'all get back. Take good care of Mista John Thomas ya heah?" "Yesum, I'll sho nuff do it." "All right 'den George Baby, you sleep good now ya heah?" "You too Momma, you too. Good night," and I kissed her pretty head gently and laid down for a long night's sleep. Was I really about to go to War? Just like that? Hmmm… maybe it won't be too bad, why just today I heard James say, "Hey fellas, Lucius from my Sunday school class told me on Sunday that he reckons we oughtta be able to whip the Yankees and be home for Christmas. His daddy told him he didn't believe it, but he does, and so do I.

What do they know about war and guns, ain't we been hunting our whole lives, and each of us can practically hit a squirrel in the eye blindfolded from half a mile. There ain't nothing to be scared about of them Yankees! They're the ones who should fear us." Lawdy, Lawdy, those boys sho were excited about going off to war. Was Mister Carson right about war? Was war truly a miserable experience? From what I can tell, I reckon he's right as rain. Children in school are taught about the long winters George Washington's men suffered during the Revolutionary War without shoes and lack of food. I reckon that don't sound too convincing to me that war is a grand experience. In fact, it sounds like something anybody with half a brain would run from it like the plague. Is the North really right? Is the South really right? Didn't the preacher talk recently about Paul's letter to the Church at Corinth? "Was any man called when he was already circumcised? He is not to become uncircumcised. Circumcision is nothing, and uncircumcision is nothing, but *what matters is* the keeping of the commandments of God. Each man must remain in that condition in which he was called. Were you called while a slave? Do not worry about it; but if you are able to become free, rather do that. For he

29

who was called in the Lord while a slave, is the Lord's Freedman; likewise he who was called while free, is Christ's slave. You were bought with a price; do not become slaves of men. Brethren, each one is to remain with God in that *condition* in which he was called." If Paul said, "he who was called in the Lawd while a slave, is the Lawd's Freedmen, and "he who was called while free is Christ's slave," I reckon that evens everything out in the end. Ain't we all going to heaven or hell, and I *KNOW* everybody's gonna be the same in either of them places, so is this really worth going to war over? Is it really? Why I know folks who tell me that Lula and I live like kings compared to a lot of black people up North. They say, "George, you got your own house, you got your own land, y'all eat like Kings thanks to Lula's delicious cooking, and if *that* ain't enough, Mister Carson takes real good care of y'all. White folks up North may "act" like they're against slavery, but try talking to one of 'em on the streets of New York City. They'll either run away to the other side of the road from ya, or say 'get out of my way boy!'"

Oh, Lawd, have mercy, what's a man to do? "Lawd, thank you again for this wonderful life you've given us. In your divine mercy, you know every thought, every action, & every word we have or ever will speak. Help us to glorify your great name in the good times and the bad, in Jesus' great name, Amen." I slept the sleep of the dead that night, not a care in the world. The rain and the cooler air helped too I reckon. After breakfast Robert and I decided to go Turkey hunting. We have a good spot we like to go to around the river. Robert just turned 15, so he was excited, and full of energy. Reckon for an old man, I was in pretty good shape still myself. "George you hear what those South Carolinians did to them Yankees at Fort Sumter?" "Yes, suh, Mister Robert, I sho nuff did. Reckon they whipped 'em pretty good huh?" "Yeah George, way I heard it, they bombed 'em out there on that little Island so rough that Major Anderson had to get some new drawers by the time he ran up that white flag!!!" Robert broke into a fit of laughing that lasted awhile 'til he was back to normal. We parked our wagon on the bank of the muddy Flint River, got off on foot, and started off to spot where we waited for our bird. Lula packed us a lunch of fried chicken, potato salad, rusk and sorghum that oughtta hold us over 'til supper. Lula made the best biscuits you ever saw, in fact, I think that's the reason we always have so many guests for Sunday dinner. Sometimes the Carson's would have guests from Macon show up unannounced for Sunday dinner, but they were always shown the finest Southern hospitality, and never once did the Carson's or even Lula mind. "George, you reckon this War's gonna be over by Christmas? That's what James said." "Reckon I don't know, Mister Robert. Since I ain't never been in a war myself, but I've heard they sometimes last a long time." "Hmph" sighed Robert, "George, I hadn't told this to Pop or any of my brothers yet, but I'd kind of like to go to war with 'em one day!" "But you're just a boy, Mister Robert, you're only 15 years old. Seems like just yesterday when you were born. Yes, suh, I ain't seen your Mother and Father that happy in a long time! You shoulda seen the look on their faces when you came into this world. See they wasn't sure whether you'd be a boy or a girl.

'Course your daddy was hoping you'd be a boy, and 'course your Momma was hoping for a girl, and she sure was happy you were born though. If all y'all go off to war and get killed, what do you reckon that's gonna do to your Momma and Daddy? "Aw George, we ain't gonna get killed. That's what we're gonna do to the Yankees! Don't you see? My friend Lamar told me that Robert E. Lee is gonna raise an Army of Northern Virginia, and ain't gonna stop until he lands on the door steps of the White House itself!" "Go on, Mister Robert, how you talk, I mean it would be nice if he could do that and all y'all could be back home by Christmas, but I've lived a long time on this earth, and the one thing I've learned is that when two Armies want to fight against each other with everything they got, it's usually going to last awhile. I don't want y'all to go up there and get hurt by them Yankees, Robert. Don't you see son? Wars are very dangerous, and they're not all that glorious the way they're thought of by young towheads like yourself." "I know it might be dangerous, George, 'course I do. But don't you see, they're telling us we're wrong for how live our lives down here in the Deep South when we ain't never said nothing to 'em about how they live up there! Them Yankees think they know *everything* and as far as I can make of it they don't know nothing! What do you make of it?" "I reckon I don't make anything of it since I've never been up North. My whole life has been lived here in the great state of Georgia! Why once after you were born your Father took me up to Atlanta, and Lawd have mercy! If New York, or Boston, or Chicago were half as nice as it I'd like to see it! Anyway Mister Robert, Lula and I have lived a great life working for your father all this time. He gave us our own home, and our own land, and there's nothing better for a man, I don't care what he looks like, than to own his own home, and *his own land*." A turkey was coming around the corner right as I said this, and Robert and I both got quiet and focused our attention on it.

It ended up being one of the two birds that we bagged. Robert and I have as much fun hunting together as I often did with his three older brothers when they were his age. Hopefully the war will over with by the time he's old enough to go and fight.

He's only 15 now, so hopefully I reckon the war will be over by then. Lawd have mercy, ain't he just a itchin to go to Virginia and kill Yankees. Lawd help me talk some sense in that boys skull, 'cause I reckon there ain't much in there right now. By the time we got back to the Carson House everyone was getting ready for supper, so I told Robert to go wash up, and I'd take care of the turkeys. "Thanks, George, it's always grand hunting with ya!" "Enjoyed it as always Mister Robert, now don't get Mizz Martha upset at the supper table over all that tommyrot on killing Yankees ya heah?" "Yes Suh!" With War on the horizon, Mizz Martha didn't look too happy about the prospects of her three oldest boys going off to war, and you could tell it on her face. Every time I see her these days she puts up a good front, but I know that it's eating her alive inside. Mister Carson told me just the other day that she stirs, tosses, and turns in her sleep all night long. He can tell she's having nightmares over her boys going off to war and leaving them all alone to fend for themselves. He said that's if she sleep at all. Some nights he says she'll sit in the corner in her rocking chair with her Bible clutched to her chest, close her eye's and just pray in that chair all night long. A stranger from Montezuma might not have the slightest clue that she's worrying up inside, but everyone who knows her well can tell. Last week Mizz Martha told Lula, "Lula, they can take my first three boys from me, but thank God almighty that Robert is too young to go off to that blasted war!!!" "Yessum, ain't dat de truth. Hopefully by time dat no count wuh be over, we all be right back heah at Carson House as a family, way the good Lawd 'spect us to be." Mister Carson told me that whenever Mizz Carson is in one of her dark moods, Lula is 'bout the only one who can cheer her up. "Mister Carson, whenever I'm in a dark mood my Lula only makes it *worse!*" Mister Carson slapped his knees and let out a belly laugh the likes I ain't seen of him in 30 years. "You know George,

I expect you're right. My Pop told me that sometimes he thought that my Momma cared about everybody in the world but him sometimes. But then he told me something I've never forgotten. "Joseph that being said, don't ever forget that there is nothing better in this world than to be loved by a woman. Nothing!" Reckon he's right George, gotta take the good with bad, just like they do with us. George do you remember from Church how God created woman?" "Yes Suh, I remember the story about paradise in the Garden of Eden." "Yes, well a fella told me once that the Good Lord came to Adam in the Garden of Eden and said, "Adam, I've got the perfect helper for you. She will cook for you, clean up after you, and take real good care of you. "Adam said, "That sounds great Lord. How soon can she be here?"

"Well, that's the thing Adam, there will be a big cost attached to her." "How much will it cost me?" "Well, it's going to cost you an arm and a leg." Adam thought about it and said, "What can I get for a rib?" Now I was the one chuckling up a storm. "That's a good one, Suh, real funny." Even Mister Carson chuckled at his own joke. "George, I reckon you ought not tell Lula that if you know what's good for ya." "No Suh! No Suh! Those words shall never be uttered in my home."

After supper, I went out onto my porch and sat and looked at all the rows and rows of freshly planted cotton. Lawd it's pretty to see a freshly planted field in the spring, and to enjoy the beautiful Georgia sunsets! It always almost takes my breath away to see those amazing red Georgia sunsets. One time I read in Harper's Weekly "red sky at night sailor's delight, red sky in the morn, sailor be warned." I stuffed my pipe with some of that good Ole Virginny tobacco Mister Carson gave me and puffed away while watching the sunset. Pretty soon it'll be time to go off to war with John Thomas. Tomorrow I'll go have a talk with him and see what his thoughts are about this upcoming war. Hopefully he's got a much better perspective than Robert, and I'm sure he does. He's clerk over at First Baptist Church in Reynolds, and he and Mizz Susan have 7 children now. Unlike Robert, he's a grown man, and has responsibilities a 15 year old doesn't have.

"Good morning Mister John, how are ya, Suh?" "Fine, George, what brings you out this way? We just got through with breakfast, can I get you anything?"

"No Suh, no thank you. Lula say's I'm getting too round in my belly, so I'm trying to watch how much I eat so I don't have to hear her nag me about it all the time." John Thomas laughed out loud! "Ain't it the truth George? You got that right! Just the other day Susan told me how proud of me she was for giving her all her beautiful babies, then yesterday she told me I was the worst Daddy ever when I whipped Albert for sassing his teacher. She said I was too hard on him. Then said, "That poor thing can't sit down at the supper table without a pillow in his chair." So I said, "Serves him right.

It'll remind him not to sass his elders!" You know George, it's funny how history repeats itself. Pop whipped me more times than I can remember, and thinking back on it, I deserved every one of them, *though at the time I didn't think so.*" He smiled at that, and so did I. "What's on your mind, George? Pop tells me you volunteered to go up to Virginia with me, and I reckon I never did get the chance to thank you for it. So, for what it's worth, thank you, George." John Thomas has always been one of my favorite Carson boys. Maybe it's 'cause he's the oldest, or perhaps because he and I bonded so well when he was young. Who knows why, Lawd knows I love all them rascals, and they know it. "My pleasure suh, happy to do it." "You want to go for a walk and enjoy this beautiful morning the good Lord has blessed us with?" "Yes, suh, that would be nice." We walked up River

Road in the direction of Reynolds. Luckily it rained a little last night, so we weren't choked in clay dust. John Thomas had grown into a fine gentleman. Reckon he was about six feet tall and strong as an ox. Every time at school his buddies would want to race he would always win. ALWAYS. Can't say I ever remember him losing one foot race. Reckon when he was twelve one day he said he wanted to race me home, so I said okay, and "on your mark, get set, GO!!!" It was only about a quarter mile home, but before I knew it he was already there and I still had 50 yards to go! "Come on, George, you're almost there." I was so out of breath when I got finished I had to catch my breath for what seemed an eternity but probably was only 10 minutes. I remember that day often, and fondly. "Boy, where'd you learn how to run that fast?" "At school, George." "How? I ain't that old, and I ain't never lost a foot race in my whole life before today." "Oh don't worry George, I didn't have a choice. See when we were at recess one day, me and Miss Susan went behind the school house, and I told her she was the prettiest thing I had ever seen, and I wanted to kiss her. Well, she said thank you and I could kiss her, but only if it was on the cheek where her Momma made her brother kiss her.

So right when I was done kissing her cheek I hear this gorilla yell out, "HEY BOY, WHAT IN TARNATION YOU DOING TO MY SISTER?!!" It was her older brother Jethro, and he was with 5 of his friends, and, George, they were all a head taller than me and twice as big, so I did the only thing I could think of. I ran! I ran, and ran, and ran. Every now and then I'd look behind me, but before I knew it I couldn't see 'em anymore. Realizing I was almost at the River, I turned around and jogged back to the school house through the woods different than the way I'd run from 'em. The rest of the afternoon I kept hearing 'em snicker in class and say, "We're gonna get you John Thomas after school and bloody your lip." So when Miss Johnson asked if anyone would like to volunteer to get wood for the stove for tomorrow, my hand shot up and I said, "I'll do it Miss Johnson." Well, I rounded up a ton of wood the first time I went out, and when I came back, there was almost enough wood to fill the entire stove for a whole week of school, but I said, "I think you need a little more, Miss Johnson," and when I went outside I ran the whole mile all the way home instead of going back inside. After that, Jethro and his friends tried to catch me at recess, but they never did. I reckon that's how I got to be such a fast runner." "Well, that's great, John Thomas. Just make sure they never catch you kissing his sister again."

"George, the Yankees are backing us into a corner, and I reckon the only thing we can do is fight our way out of it. I know a lot of those local hotheads are anxious to go and fight the blasted Yankees who are threatening our way of life. I don't understand why they can't just live the way they do up in Boston and New York, and leave us alone." "I know, Mister Carson, that I can't say I understand it either." We walked on in silence a bit, enjoying the fields, and the warm sunshine on our backs.

"Look at these beautiful fields, and all these fine homes we live in. I cannot imagine the Yankees coming down here and stealing our homes and our land from us It isn't right, George. It isn't right, and that's why I signed up for the 12th Georgia Regiment. Not to kill Yankees like those young hotheads want to, but to protect our way of life. If they can't understand that, then we'll take the fight to *them!* When you get down to it George, nobody wants to go to war. Maybe those dandies up in Washington and Richmond who sit behind a desk, and will never have to carry a load, or get shot at, think they know what's right for everybody else. All the gentlemen I've talked to here and in Reynolds say they'd much rather stay here than go up North for a protracted period of time, and be away from their wives and children. However, they understand that Washington has drawn a line in the sand, and we mustn't back down if our way of life is to survive. Everything I've heard about the North is that they are an industrial economy, while we are an agrarian economy. To survive here we need to farm, and we don't need anybody from Illinois telling us how to run our farm down here in Georgia. Last time I checked nobody from the South has gone up to Illinois, or New York, or Massachusetts and told them how to run *their* farms, or *their* factories. No suh, that's not how we operate down here and why for the life of me they want to meddle in our affairs is a burr in my saddle. We might not have as many troops as they do, and we might not enjoy some of their fancy weaponry, but we have something those Yankees will never have, and that, suh, is fidelity to the spirit of our cause, for we know if we lose, our entire way of life will forever be different."

Mister Carson was right of course. What would the South be if it weren't for agriculture, and slaves to run it? I have no idea, though often the thought has crossed my mind. Would the planters have enough money to pay all their servants in cash instead of land, houses, &

food? This is the only life I've ever known, and it's been a good one. I reckon I'm blessed to get to work for Mister Carson and have such a lovely wife as Lula and all the children she has blessed us with. And the land and the house Mister Carson has so graciously given our family.

Lawd have mercy! Sometimes I wish those Yankees could see that our way of life down here isn't how they portray it in Harper's Weekly.

Anyway, this is the only life I've ever known, and, Lawd, you have blessed it. Thank you, Lawd! "Mister Carson, you reckon we're gonna be up there fighting awhile or be home for Christmas. I reckon I need to know what to pack." "Not quite sure, George, I wish I could say we'd be home for Christmas, but if I had my druthers I'd say we'll be up there for a good while. What I heard is General Lee wants to invade Pennsylvania and Washington D.C. one day! Lord have mercy. George, I don't know how realistic that is, but what if General Lee could do that, get *them* to surrender by Christmas, and leave us alone? Why, that would be grand I reckon. The best advice I could give you would be to pack all your summer clothes, and your winter clothes, and don't forget your rifle and your hunting knife." "Nobody's gonna mind me carrying a rifle, suh?" "Naw George, you're gonna be with me as my porter, and nobody's going to question why the porter of a commissioned officer of the C.S.A. is carrying a rifle with him. They'll probably think it's mine anyhow. Besides, there's gonna be a lot of mouths to feed up there, and you never know, we might have to hunt us up something to eat sometime. Napoleon said, "An Army marches on its stomach," and there's gonna be a whole lot of stomachs marching, so yeah, bring your rifle, your hunting knife, and whatever else you think we might need." "Very good, suh, when you reckon we'll be departing? I'm sure Lula would like to cook us up a fine meal before we take off for Ole Virginny." "Indeed, George, nobody can pass up a gourmet supper from Georgia's finest cook can they?" "No suh, indeed not. You know once your father told me a friend of his from Atlanta took a "detour" here on the way to Savannah just to eat supper at his table." "You don't say? I knew she had a lot of admirers, but I don't reckon I heard that tale before. You got quite a wife there, George." "Thank you, suh."

We walked along the road enjoying the view. Hopefully this would all be the same when we get home from up North, heaven only knows. If the Lawd's willing, and the creek don't rise I guess. "Mister John, what do you want to do when you get home from the war?" "Same thing I've always done, George, farm. To get up in the morning and see the sunrise on your own land, work a full days' work in the field, and then watch it set in the evening on your own land is sublime. I reckon I have not the foggiest idea, George, how those folks live like they do up North, do you? I mean really, who would want to live in some hovel in New York City with the whole building slap full of folks? Would you? I wouldn't. Read that in Harper's Weekly recently. They build all these big buildings up there in the city, and then make the apartment rooms so tiny that only a rat would be comfortable in them. No suh, no suh. Peace & quiet, & serenity George, this is the life for me. George, are you anxious for the war to be over quick?" "Yes suh, I reckon I am, and to get back home to Lula since she can't write, I'm going to have to get somebody else to read my letters to her, and that's all right and all, suh, but, I'd rather her hear what I have to say than somebody else telling her what I said." "I understand George some things are better said between man and wife, and not through an interpreter."

"George, my Pop owns almost all of the land between here and the river as you know. If the Yankees win, I'm sure they'll take it from him, and then we won't have anywhere to live. What kind of justice is that? Surrendering our land over a war they started? No suh, no suh, they won't get my Daddy's land, not if me or my brothers have anything to say about it." "Mister Carson, do you happen to know if we'll be leaving soon or not leave for a few months?" "We're not quite sure yet George, however, I reckon it will definitely be sooner rather than later. Colonel Gordon was over for supper the other night, and he thinks we'll be leaving for Virginia in as little as a few weeks." "Very good, suh, that should give me plenty of time to pack, and get my affairs in order before we go." "I agree, George, my trunk's already packed, just sitting in our bedroom ready to go. Susan's a fine woman she'll be able to take care of the children while I'm gone, though I'm sure there will be some challenges.

She said doesn't want me to go but respects my feelings and understands everything that is at stake. Lula is a fine woman, and she'll be more than able to care of herself and mother while we're gone."

With that, we started walking back to his house, and he showed me his sword that he had just received. It was made in Solingen, Germany he said. All the officers of C.S.A would have one he proclaimed admiringly as he took it from its sheath and showed it to me. "That's a real fine looking sword, Mister Carson, can't say I've ever seen anything like it." "Thank you George, nor have I." "Yes suh, well thanks for our little chat Mister John, I enjoyed it." "Likewise, George, we'll talk more later, good day."

As I got home I couldn't get over the look and feel of that sword Mister Carson prided himself over. Why I bet there hadn't been a sword that fancy since King David took Goliath's sword in Israel that fateful day.

At home I began to pack for our journey up North. Since Mister Carson said to take pretty much everything, that's what I did. First, I grabbed that old empty steamer trunk laying in the closet collecting dust. As I went thru our chest 'o drawers, I began packing all the warm wool socks I could find for when it gets cold, as well as every pair of long john's I own. It's springtime now, so I won't be needing 'em for a while anyhow. "Lawd, help me to take good care of Mister Carson and bring him back home safe and sound to his folks, his beautiful wife, Susan, and his seven handsome children. Thank you, Lawd, in your son's name, Amen." After that, I found an extra night lamp, my tobacco pouch, and writing papers, and a pen. Next I found that old wool blanket that kept us warm during some of those freezing nights in January where the only thing that kept us from freezing to death at night was the fire in our bedroom and that old wool blanket. I found some gloves, and mufflers to help block the wind. Next, I have several hats, and I threw a few in there.

Next inside went my extra pair of boots, and I was wearing my other pair. Last I threw in some soap, and a brush to wash up with. Deciding I'll finish the rest later, I went over to Carson the House to find Robert.

"Hey, Robert, you want to go out and look for a deer?" "Sure, George, I just got done with school and had lunch, so let's go. Where do you want to go? Our normal spot?" "Yes, suh, we always get lucky over there, and we haven't had any good venison in a while, so I figure we're due. Grab your rifle, and I'll meet you out by the wagon." After I got my rifle, I went out to hook up the mule to the wagon, and when I was done here came Robert bounding down the steps of the Carson House. "All right, George, I'm all set." "Fine, fine, Mister Robert, you ready to get us a 10 point buck?" "You know it George!" We went and sat in our spot where we normally can see 1 or 2 deer come if we wait long enough. This is the spot you'll remember where Mister James dang near got him and me railroaded years ago. "George, who you reckons' gonna win the War, us or the Yankees?" "Reckon I don't rightly know, Mister Robert. Some folks say we will, some say the Yankees have so many men and supplies that they'll be able to outlast and outfight us. One thing I do know for sure is I don't want y'all to go off and get yerselves all kilt. Your Mom and Pop'll have a fit if that happens. War's a dangerous business Mister Robert. Nobody wins eventually, 'cause sometimes even if you win in a war, you lose. Remember in our Revolutionary War there were a lot of fine men killed that never got to see their families again. You gotta see past your nose, son. I know you dream every night of going up to Pennsylvania and killing Yankees, but, don't you reckon there was a boy your age just last night dreaming about killing Johnny Rebels like you?" "Don't reckon I ever thought much of it that way, George. That's something to think about for sure. John Thomas has already enlisted in the Confederate Army, 12th Georgia Regiment as you know, and y'all are getting ready to go up to Virginia to kill Yankees. James is talking about enlisting, as well as Joseph. Pop won't let me enlist dangit!!! Says I'm gonna have to wait 'til I'm a man. I say I'm already a man, can do a full day's work same as anybody else.

But he says, "No suh, no way, no how are you going off to War until you're 18 boy." "Well, I said, 'yes suh Pop.' But, I can't wait to go, George. That'll mean I'll have to wait 3 years George, and the war'll be over by then, and I won't have killed nothing but time." We just sat there for a while and stared at the pretty Georgia countryside, rolling hills on top of red Georgia clay and Georgia Pines. We could sit out here for hours at a time in perfect peace. The preacher man on Sunday said in Israel, Shalom stands for peace. "Pray for the peace of Jerusalem" he said as the Psalm says. Lawd, it sure is peaceful here though. What will the war do to this peace? Will the Yankees come and destroy it and us at the same time? Lawd I hope not. Robert's thoughts varied from leading a cavalry charge against the Northerners, to pushing 'em back across the Mason Dixon line where they belong, or to launching an artillery barrage against 'em for days, and nigh on months at a time. All those thoughts would hopefully one day never come true, for Robert Hall Carson was the apple of his folk's eyes. Born almost 21 years after his eldest brother John Thomas, I suspect he was an accident. Nothing wrong with that, it happens to folks all the time. Whether the Carson's planned for him, or not, there was no way Mister and Mizz Carson were going to let their youngest child Robert go off to War without a fight themselves. Luckily for 'em, like Robert said, hopefully the war will be over by the time he's of age. Nonetheless, we heard rumors already that half the Yankee fighting men were rumored to be under the age of 18 already, and so had Robert. In spite of this, he's a good boy, and wants to honor and please his folks, so when they told him couldn't go fight, he took it in stride and said "Yessum, yes suh." "George, George, I think I see 10 Deer! No, it's 15!" I took a gander over where he was looking, and I'll be darned if there weren't that many. Land sakes alive! There were more deer in that herd than I've ever seen in a pack before. We were sitting up on a bluff overlooking the river plain. To our backs the sun was going down, and it was so low in the sky that if the deer turned to look, they wouldn't see us, but the bright sun in their eyes. This was gonna be like shooting fish in a barrel! On the other side of the deer was the river, so the only way they could run was right or left. "Robert, hold still now, and breathe easy."

"All right George, I'll do it." "Now Mister Robert, here's what we're gonna do. You see that Crepe Myrtle tree yonder by the river?" "Yeah, George, I see it." He was on my right, and I was on his left. The commanding view of our targets was incredible! We were no more than 90 yards away from all those beautiful bucks, and I could hardly contain my excitement. "Okay, Mister Robert, you shoot anything to the right of the Crape Myrtle, and I'll shoot anything to the left of it. I suggest you shoot from the outside and work your way back in. If they don't all scatter in the same direction, which I suspect they won't, then that should give us time to hopefully get maybe 4 or 5 of 'em. Now get good and sighted in." Both of us got prone on the ground and used our elbows to tightly get perfect sights on our targets. If only the Yankees provided such good targets for our boys as these deer did. The deer had no idea this was gonna be their last day on this beautiful Georgia clay. "Mister Robert you got a good sight picture?" "I do, George." "Okay, so do I whenever you're ready, fire." Before the word was completely out of my mouth, the explosion of his rifle filled my ears, and I saw the big buck on the far right go down. Meanwhile, I sighted in on the one I was shooting at and shot him through the heart. Before I was done reloading another explosion rang out in the air, and Robert had dropped himself another big buck. After quickly reloading, I shot another one on the far left, and after that all the rest of the herd had vanished. That was okay though since the four we did hit were huge! The two Robert hit looked upwards of 200lbs!!! And the two I hit didn't look much smaller than that. "I'll go get the wagon Mister Robert, and I'll be right back." After I got the wagon, & we loaded it up with all four of those big bucks we was slap wore out! Robert and I enjoyed a little small talk on the way home, and by the time we arrived back home, everybody was thrilled over our catch! Mister Robert went on to wash up for supper, while I took the deer out back of the house to be field dressed. After supper, Lula and I sat out on the front porch and looked at the beautiful cotton fields that dotted our view. Tomorrow was the Sabbath, and we had to be up early to get everybody ready for Church.

After Church Mister Carson and I went out back and walked along the fields and looked at all the rows after rows of cotton there were. "Pretty good sermon today huh, George?" "Yes Suh, I reckon so." "Reverend Glover was down right indignant about them Yankees huh?" "Yes Suh, that was the most fire I've ever seen come out of the reverend's belly since he started preaching to us, what about a year ago suh?" "Yes, about a year now. Before today I've never heard him so much as raise his voice before." "This War is GONNA TEAR OUR NATION APART!" The Reverend bellowed. "Mister Lincoln calls himself a Christian, but how can he when threatens to exterminate good Christian men who are his brothers, but, unfortunately for them they live below the Mason-Dixon line! This nation cannot...CANNOT FIGHT AGAINST ITSELF, AND BE BLESSED BY THE ALMIGHTY!!! NO SUH! IT WILL NOT BE BLESSED BY PROVIDENCE IF IT CHOOSES TO MAKE A PACT WITH THE DEVIL AND KILL EACH OTHER OVER STATES RIGHTS!!! Did the nation of Israel remain standing when they entered into a bloody civil war? No suh it did not! Only 7,000 remained in Israel who had not bowed unto Baal! 7,000 men! "Yet I have left me seven thousand in Israel, all the knees which have not bowed unto Baal, and every mouth which hath not kissed him." How did their civil war help Israel prosper brothers? Answer, it did not. Soon after this the good Lord deported them to Babylon, and King Nebuchadnezzer sacked the Holy City of Jerusalem until it was destroyed because of brother bearing arms against brother! I understand soon young men from

Taylor, Macon, Muscogee, and all other counties are soon leaving their beloved wives and families soon… FOR WHAT?!! TO GO KILL THEIR NORTHERN CHRISTIAN BROTHERS??? Lord have mercy!" The firery preacher took of his spectacles and wiped them with his handkerchief. When he was finished he took a deep breath, and in his normal, sedate voice said, "Please stand. Let us pray. Almighty God, maker of heaven and earth we beseech thee Lord. Help us in our hour of need, and come down and protect our nation as only you can dear Lord. We pray for our dear President Lincoln, Lord give him wisdom in how to lead our country to peace, and prosperity. We pray for Mr. Davis up in Richmond, dear Lord, give him the strength, and thy wisdom to reconcile our nation with our Northern brothers. Lord Jesus, you assure us in your scripture that, "Verily I say unto you, whatsoever ye shall bind on earth shall be bound in heaven: and whatsoever ye shall loose on earth shall be loosed in heaven." Lord help us to rebind our nation as it were at the beginning Father. May our hearts be turned to you and not to hate. Help us to love our Northern brethren like you love thy Church Lord. Be with these boys of the Confederate Army Lord, send your angel Gabriel unto them to watch their backs, and protect them from the wiles of the devil. Father in heaven, we beseech thy great name to be with our brethren up North, may they not hate us Father, nor us them, but may Northern brother of Christ be reconciled with his Southern brother of Christ very soon. Dear Lord be with the families of these soldiers as they deploy up North, take care of them while their men are gone, and provide for their needs Father through this Church and their families. In the almighty name of Jesus Christ, we ask these things, Lord, Amen.

"Yes, Suh, I reckon he was a tad fired up today." Mister Carson chuckled, he was on the search committee to find the new preacher and had been assured that he was not a screamer, like the last one was. Some Sabbaths there wasn't a soul to be seen on the first three rows for fear of their ear drums bursting. Well, I reckon that only made it worse since the Preacher felt that with the people sitting farther away, he had to yell even *louder*.

Now with our new Pastor, people are back up to the front pews. "George, I reckon the **times have got the Preacher genuinely upset, can you blame him? Why Miss Martha is worried** sick over her boys, and this blasted War that's creeping toward them day by day. What I wouldn't give for everything to be normal, like it was before all those rabble rousers up North started raising Cain about 5 or 10 years ago." Yes, suh, remember them days like they was yesterday. The thing is, we're out in the country, far away from any big towns. Even now with all that's going on in the world when we're at home it's like nothing's ever changed at all. Now if we were to go into town at Reynolds, then everybody would be all stirred up about the war and all, and that's all they'd want to talk about."

"George, have you got all your gear packed up to go off with John Thomas?" "Yes suh, finished packing last night." "Good, well 1st Lt. Carson tells me he's all packed up and ready to go. George, since he ain't no spring chicken anymore, pushing 36 years old this fall, he isn't as excited about this War as Robert is. However, he feels he's doing his duty for his people. We know you'll take great care of him, as we will of Lula." "Thank you, suh, I know y'all will take great care of her, just beware of her temper. At the drop of a hat that women can plunge into a bilious humor the likes of which you never saw." Mister Carson silently laughed, he'd seen me endure Lula's wrath going on 40 years. When I was first married to her he gave me some great marriage advice. He said,

"George, whenever your wife is scolding you when it's not your fault, just nod your head and say, "Yes dear. Sorry, dear." "Yes suh that has worked rather well over most of the last 40 years. Except for the time way back when, when John Thomas and James lit Besses tail on fire. Lawd I reckon I heard about that for a month!" Lula will provide great care for Mister and Mizz Carson, and the good Lawd couldn't have blessed 'em with a more capable helper.

"I reckon y'all will be leaving soon George, and there's something I want to give you before you go." He reached into his vest pocket and pulled out his gold pocket watch, the one I've seen him wear every day I've known him for the last 40 years. Clasped inside his right hand, he pushed his arm forward and handed it to me. "Take it George. My Daddy John Wesley Carson gave it to me when I turned 21 many years ago." I was thunderstruck! No servant has ever owned a watch! At least not one I've ever known. I looked on the back, and it said,

Joseph Jefferson Carson
Happy 21st Birthday
4/16/1823

Well, I'll be, Mister Carson wants to give me a watch his Pop gave him for his 21st birthday! "Thank you suh, I'm at a loss for words, and I can't thank you enough for this beautiful gift." "You're welcome George, indeed, that's *the least* I felt I should do for you for all you've done for my boys. They all adore you, and have fond memories of all their time spent playing and hunting with you, and I don't know why, but Robert seems to admire you even more than his brothers do. George, I hear rumors that John Thomas' Company C, Davis Rifles outfit is about to depart." He reached out to shake my hand, and then he took my hand in both of his and said, "George, take good care of John Thomas and bring him back to me please." "Yes, suh, I'll take real good care of him, don't you worry now you hear, suh. We'll be fine." Mister Carson smiled a tired smile, took a couple of puffs from his briar pipe, and we walked lazily back to the house. As he was about to go back into the house, he came back down the porch and stood in front of me, and again took my right hand in his, and said, "George, no matter what…no matter what happens to my boy, bring…bring him back to me and his family, George." Mister Carson seemed a little upset, Lawd can you blame him? His oldest boy was about to go to war, and the rest of his sons were chomping at the bit to go as well. Reckon he had a lot on his heart this day. "Yes suh, I'll bring him back to you suh, no matter what." "Thank you George. Thank you so much for your fidelity to me and my boys," and then he turned to go inside the house.

Chapter 3

With that I turned to go back to my house. Lula was waiting for me when I stepped in the door. "George, honey, what Mista Carson have to say?" "Oh, Baby, he's concerned about John Thomas. You can see it all over his face. To top that, you know that gold pocket watch he has?" "Sho do, dat's de prettiest watch in de county!" I took it out of my pocket and showed it to her. "George, what in de world you doing holding dat? Mista Carson find out he'll have yo hide!" "That's what I'm trying to tell you Baby, he gave it to *me. Me!!!* Reckon I still don't know why he did it. No idea at all. No ma'am. He insisted that I take it, so I did." "George what 'dat say on de back?"

Joseph Jefferson Carson
Happy 21ˢᵗ Birthday
4/16/1823

"It says, "Joseph Jefferson Carson. Happy 21ˢᵗ Birthday, April 16ᵗʰ 1823." "Lawd have mercy. We weren't much older dan Mister Robert back den. George, honey, why'd he give 'dat to you again?" "Told you Baby, I don't rightly know and tried to give it back, but he insisted I take it. He wanted me to have it! He's probably got 10 others just like it."

"Dat ain't de point, George! When de last time you ever see a servant with a watch like dat?" "I reckon I never have before." "Dat's right Baby! Either Mista Carson gone senile, or he really to up bout Mista John Thomas. Lawd have mercy! You remember when dat boy's born how happy dat man was over his first son?!! Land sakes chile, he weren't much older dan Joseph is now. How he used to sit up dere on dat porch and play with dat chile for hours a time. Now he bout to go up to Virginny and get kilt no doubt by some Ragamuffin, no count Yankee scoundrels! George, you goin take good care of him ain't ya? I know you is, but, George, you know John Thomas already in de Army, and James talking about get in hisself also, along with Joseph as well. Lawd George! It tearing Mista and Mizz Carson's heart out!!! They don't think nobody can tell, but I can. The other day while I be cooking supper, Mizz Carson tell Mista Carson if her boys don't come back from this blasted war she doan know if she wanta live anymo. And now Mister Robert, he something else! Last night I hear him tell Joseph soon as he turn 18 he gonna go help his brothers kill Yankees! Ain't dat something? He oughtta be ought courting dem pretty girls at de Church, but nooooooooooooo. All he talk bout is Yankee dis, Yankee dat. Every time he eat now he say, "give me double Mizz Lula, I got get big and strong so I can help my brothers kill Yankees." Lawd have mercy, every time he say dat Mister & Mizz Carson dey doan say nothing, dey jess listen. Mista Lincoln goan free all de slaves after dem Yankees win de Wuh! George, what you make of it?" "I don't make anything of it Baby. Free or not free, how you reckon its gonna be any different for *us?* We've got our own house, our *own* land out back, and our own garden. We eat everyday like kings and queens, thanks in no small part to your wonderful cooking." Lawd have mercy, Lula smiled, and by golly I believe she was actually blushing. We got beautiful children, and beautiful grandchildren. More than we can keep up with huh?

"The good Lawd's been real good to us Lula, so I can't see how it's gonna make much difference for us really.

Now it will make a difference for other folks I reckon, but not us, Honey. This is our home here in the great state of Georgia!" "Yeah, Baby, reckon you probably right. Some dem rascals out in de field oh how they talk. Lawd! They talk bout being free, and dey say dey can't wait to be free, and I say, Why you fool! What difference dat be between you now, and you den? All dis talk bout being free, and you ain't got no idea how you good you got it heah with de Carson's. Mister Carson take real good care y'all, and he ain't never raised his voice to y'all, nuther lessen one of you rascals deserved it. Y'all ain't never been hungry a day in your lives, not one!" "Lawd, George, dey get me upset dey do." "Don't worry about 'em Baby, they're field hands, all they know is what they hear from other folks when they're gossiping. Almost every one of them works hard, and never sasses Mister Carson. Lawd, they know better than that. Baby, Mister Carson and me have talked a lot the last few years about what will happen after the war if the Yankees win. He said there's a chance they could take our land and property as reparations for the war." "Repertions, what in de world is dat Honey?" "Well, Baby, it's when they make the loser of a war pay the winner for the cost of the war. He told me years ago they'd probably take our house and land too if they win. Can you believe that Honey? After coming to *free us, they loot us.* That be the case, they can just stay up there, thank you very much. Reckon we're doing fine on our own, and don't need no help from Mister Lincoln." Lula sat there with a look of horror over her face and just stared at me with a blank expression that I've never seen from her before in all the many years we've been married. She sat there like that, silent as a ghost for 5 whole minutes in our silent house. "And take *our* land George? Fo what??? We ain't never done nothing to no Yankee! Heah dey come to free us, den dey take everything we worked our whole life fo, now if dat make any sense at all I be de Queen of Sheba!"

"It's all right, Dear, I reckon everyone's upset right now. You saw how worked up the Preacher was today at Church, and I figured all the planters in *Georgia are just as upset as he was at having to give up one or more of their blasted sons to go and fight in this silly war!"*

All these silly young men like Mister Robert think war's glorious, and they need to prove their honor, and this and that silly notion seem not to understand that there's a good chance they might not come back from this war. They don't understand there's folks back here worried sick about 'em, and not knowing how they're getting along for months at a time, while their up there fighting Yankees." "George when you go up dere you take good care of Mista John, but Baby make sho you take good care of *you!* Doan want no dadblame Yankee taking my good husband de good Lawd give me years ago. George, I pray fo you and Mista John Thomas while you gone, and I know the good Lawd he'll bring y'all back safe and sound." "Thank you, Baby, we'll definitely need your prayers, and all the prayers of everyone else." I went over and gave her a hug. "Everything's gonna be all right, Baby. Everything's gonna be fine, Honey. The good Lawd has blessed this life of ours, and he'll take care of his children." "It ain't y'all I'ma worried about Honey, it's de Yankees! I'm afraid of what y'all gone do to *dem!*"

Around 3 o'clock I rode over to John Thomas' house to see how he was doing. "Hey there George, good to see you." "You too, Mister John, just came by to see if you've heard anything about when we're leaving." "No, I haven't George, but everybody's saying it'll be soon. Real soon. Why don't you swing by in the morning, and then you can come with me over to Marshallville, and watch the troops drill. Perhaps Captain McMillan might know more about when we're deploying up to Virginia." "That sounds good, Mister John. I'll see you in the morning at sunrise." "Look forward to it George. See you then."

As I rode home I had the itchy feeling that we were gonna be leaving sooner than we thought. Last month those South Carolinians threw Major Anderson and his cohorts out of Fort Sumter, and things have been moving along now at lightning speed. Those states that were reluctant to secede at first have now mobilized their Armies and are getting ready for war at breakneck speed according to Harpers Weekly.

Under the leadership of Captain John McMillan, formerly a school teacher, he had organized Company C, Davis Rifles. The men had been drilling and had requisitioned Govenor Brown for uniforms and arms to train and fight with. After being outfitted, Company C was a fine looking outfit. 'Course I'd never seen a company of infantrymen before, but I reckon if I did they wouldn't look near as fierce as these Johnny Rebels. After enlisting this month as a private in the army, they quickly made John Thomas a 1st Lieutenant. Reckon they did that 'cause he's 10-15 years older than the rest of the soldiers, or maybe they did it 'cause they knew he'd

be a fine officer. Regardless, they were lucky to have him,
and he was lucky to have 'em. I knew a lot of them boys
since they was knee high to a duck, known them their
whole lives, and they were good men. Really I thought
of them as boys, but, going to war and all will turn a boy
into a man real quick I reckon.

After I got home, Lula and I sat at the kitchen table
and just made small talk. She didn't want me to go off
to war I could tell, although she knew I'd take real good
care of John Thomas and that made her happy. Knowing
that it would also make the Carson's happy as well.

Supper that night was superb! Lula made my favorite:
country fried steak, mashed potatoes, corn on the cob,
along with a host of vegetables. I didn't like vegetables,
never had.

Although after decades of marriage to this wonderful
woman I have learned to fake it when I have to. When
I was young I hated collard greens, string beans, and
broccoli! Who would make a body each such stuff? I
reckon everyone's always going on about how vegetables
is good for you and all, and my sweet grandmother
always used to say, "Yo mouth might not like 'em, but
yo stomach does!" Lawd, I always wanted to tell her,

"But Grandmomma, I'm more worried about my *mouth* than my stomach." But I didn't, out of respect for her. She loved her vegetables! And she lived to be 96 years young, and she always said it was 'cause she ate "her collard greens, peas, and cornbread." Mister Carson don't like vegetables nuther, and he always seems to be in good spirits and doesn't ever have to see the doctor, so I wonder if all that stuff about vegetables being good for you is just an old wives tale.

Oh we also had some of Lula's famous sweet rolls that were out of sight! Lawd have mercy, were they good! Now here's the best part, I didn't think she was gonna bake anything for dessert tonight, but oh was I wrong. After we had cleaned the table of all the dishes she asked me if I was ready for dessert. "Dessert?" I said, "My breeches are about to bust!" And then she pulled out a sight to these old eyes. Underneath the cabinet she pulled out a red velvet cake! Lawd have mercy! There's *always* room for red velvet cake. After supper, we talked some more on the front porch. What gnats my pipe smoke didn't run off, I got rid of the rest by blowing them away out of the side of my mouth. If you're from this part of Georgia you tolerate gnats, but you can never really get used to them. Now, if you ain't from around here, then you're probably more likely to be heaping and a hollering about them all day long. There used to be some Yankees around here named the Wilbur's. Mizz Wilbur was always complaining about gnats. "Gnats this, gnats that." Lawd that woman would go on and on, and on, and on. "We don't have gnats like this up North.

They get in every nook and cranny of your house, and they drive me crazy! I keep telling Mr. Wilbur we need to move back home to get away from these wretched gnats! I can't go outside the house without being covered by the blasted critters!" Folks around the county always laughed and laughed how if you went to visit the Wilbur's when they let you in the door, if the maid didn't shut the door exactly as soon as the guests had made it through the threshold, Mizz Wilbur was want to scream in a hysterical voice, "*CLOSE THAT BLASTED DOOR, BETTY!!! THOSE NASTY GNATS ARE SUCKING THE LIFE OUT OF ME!!!!!!!!!!!!*"

I chuckled softly at her memory. In spite of all that, Mizz Wilbur could be as kind and as gentle as any Southern lady I've ever known. It's just that, well......
Southern ladies are more careful about what they say and to whom. Reckon up North folks just say whatever's on

their mind and don't think twice about it. Never really thought about it much since I've lived here in Georgia my whole life, and the Wilbur's are really the only Yankees I've ever known well. Mister and Mizz Carson had them over to the house on several occasions, and they were both always pleasant enough to me and everyone else. I reckon with everyone being so polite and so genteel down here, after seeing Mizz Wibur's outbursts, it was kind of a shock to everyone's system at first.

Oh, Lawd, how long before John Thomas and I depart for Virginia and up North? Probably sooner than we thought I reckon. As I smoked my pipe, enjoying some of that Virginia tobacco, I was happy I'd at least be able to get it first hand up there, instead of having to wait for 'em to ship it to us here in Georgia. Even though that'll be at least one benefit of being up there, I reckoned that I like everybody else was gonna be homesick quickly.

For I'd never been away from home for more than a day or two when Mister Carson had business in Atlanta, or Macon, or even Savannah. How was I gonna make it being months and maybe years away frommy family in the years when I should be settling down, not going to war! Mister Carson needs me to take good care of John

Thomas, and I told him I'd do it, so I ain't gonna whine about it any longer.

I watched the sun set below the beautiful Georgia countryside. Smoking my pipe, and drinking my coffee, not a care in the world. What would happen in the war would happen, and it was no use worrying about it. So instead, I enjoyed the sunset over the trees. I have no idea how many sunsets I've seen in my lifetime, though I reckon it's a heap. As soon as the sun set Lula and I went to sleep. After getting a greater night of rest than I had had in longer than I could remember, I got up and got ready for breakfast. Lula was already up, and breakfast was almost ready. "Morning, George, how you sleep Baby?" "Good morning, Honey, better than I have in I don't know how long." She handed me my coffee, and I began to feel fully awake again. Some of Lula's strong coffee will do that to a body. If you're not used to it, beware. Often times Mizz Carson tells her to water it down when they entertain guests who are not used to strong coffee. Breakfast consisted of eggs, bacon, sausage, cheese grits with hash on top, and biscuits and gravy! Lawd have mercy, after over 40 years of this dear woman's cooking, Lawd, would it be possible to do another 40 years, if it be in your divine will?

"George, you going out with Mista John this morning?" "Yes, ma'am, as soon as I finish this delicious breakfast you cooked for me. Do you miss cooking for all the children all the time, now that it's just you and me, Honey, and they've grown up and have their own families to cook for?" "I never minded dat so much as all de dishes! 'Cause befo I could get 'em to help me with de dishes dey was always scattered to de wind, so I don't miss *all dem dishes*."

Maybe after the war we could open up our own restaurant if anybody has any money left, and we could earn a living off of her fantastic cooking. Lawd knows, if we lived in a big city like Atlanta we could be rich!

As I rode my favorite horse Lester over to John Thomas' house I had plenty of time to think about what the future might hold for us in the next fortnight. Pretty soon we'd be heading up to Augusta, and then straight up to Richmond, Virginia to join General Lee's forces of the Army of Northern Virginia. "Oh dear Lawd, please protect your humble servants John Thomas and me, as we head off for War. Thank you for your divine providence in all the many blessings you've given us here in Macon County. Bring us back here safe and sound after the war is over. Thank you Lord, Amen."

John Thomas' farm was about 2 miles south of our house off River Road, so I was there in less than 13 minutes, according to the pocket watch Mister Carson so generously gave me. Lester and I trotted along at an easy pace. Sometimes he wanted to speed it up, and I let him, though not as fast as he'd like to run anymore. Lester's a young horse, and has a lot of energy, so he gets most of his exercise in the pasture out back. Too bad I can't take him with me to Virginia, that's a shame. If I needed to get away from the Yankees in a hurry, he'd sure be the way to go.

As we rode up the driveway, John Thomas was already outside, and ready to go in his shiny butternut uniform. 1st Lt John Thomas Carson, 35 years old and oldest son of Joseph Jefferson Carson. Platoon Leader of Company C, 12th Georgia Regiment, "Davis Rifles." I never can remember why they're called that. I reckon it could be in honor of Jefferson Davis his own self. Don't rightly know, nobody ever explained it to me. Company A of the 12th Georgia Regiment was the "Muckalee Guards," Company B was "Jones Volunteers," Company D was "Calhoun Rifles," Company E was "Muscogee Rifles," Company F was "Davis Guards," Company G was "Putnam Light Infantry," Company H was "Central

City Blues," Company I was Lowndes Volunteers," and Co K's Marion Guards filled out the regiment.

John Thomas and I were gonna go out to Marshallville to watch the men drill, and see how they were getting along. "How'd you sleep last night, George?" "Like a baby suh, like a baby. How 'bout yourself?" "I slept all right, but Susan's having a hard time sleeping right now with the war and all. However, after I take a few sips from my swoon bottle, I have no trouble falling asleep at all." I laughed 'cause I know what he meant. When I was his age somebody once gave me a swoon bottle that was full to the top with a brown, amber colored liquid. Lula had already gone to bed that night, and so I decided to sit out on my porch, smoke my pipe, and try out this swoon bottle. The first sip I took tasted bitter and I didn't much care for it. However, right after that it put a fire in my belly that I'd never had before. Anyway, before I knew it, I had drunk half the bottle. Being in a really good mood I went inside and went to bed, happy as I ever remembered being. Until I woke up that is. "GEORGE, GEORGE, WAKE UP!!!" Lula screamed at me. "What, huh, what time is it?" "Why it's 6:30 George, WAKE UP! You overslept fo 2 hours. I was jess 'bout to pour cold water on yo head, but now I see's you's alive, so I ain't gone do it, less you don't get up right this second!" Lawd have mercy! I will never forget that morning for the rest of my life. After the fog cleared up from my head, I realized I had the worst headache I'd ever had in my life, and the day was just getting started. "George, where'd you get dat swoon bottle? You drank all dat licker last night? Didn't you?!!! You know you ain't posed to drink licker. De Preacher say you ain't posed too. Who gave you dat?" I couldn't tell her because I promised him that I wouldn't tell anyone who gave it to me, so I just said, "What, huh? Oh, that, I found it down by the river the other day when we were fishing." "Um huh, no wonder you slept so long, and look like you got a headache. De Preacher say dat stuff looks good in de bottle, but when it go in yo belly it make yo head see strange things." Lula's preaching only made my head hurt worse, so I quickly dressed, as quickly as I could that day and went out to meet Mister Carson. We were going hunting at 7, and I believe I got there at 6:59. "Good morning George," Mister Carson said as brightly and warmly as he could. "Good morning suh."

"George, you don't look so well this morning, did you take a little sip out that swoon bottle I gave you last night?" "Yes suh, except for the fact that when I was done

I realized I had nearly drank half the bottle." Mister Carson laughed, and laughed, and laughed. "George I told you to go easy on that stuff since you'd never had any before." "Yes suh, I know, it's just that I wasn't paying attention to anything after my first few sips, and then by the time I went to bed I had drank half the bottle." Mister Carson laughed some more. "I reckon you must have quite a headache, huh?" "Indeed, suh, worst one I ever had." Mister Carson chuckled to himself, then said, "George, make sure you fill up four canteens of water for yourself for today instead of your normal two, and make *sure* you drink every bit of that water today, and while you're doing that, I'll go get you some Castor Oil." I heard him laugh and chuckle as he headed back inside the house. After taking my medicine and drinking two full canteens of water, the pounding in my head had stopped. Thank you, oh Lawd for that!!! "George, they call that sipping Bourbon. You ain't supposed to chug it Gentlemen sip it on their porches or in their libraries in the wintertime. You gotta take it easy on that stuff, or it'll make you pay for it as you found out." "Yes suh, thank you for the advice, suh!"

"Other than that, Mister John, how's Mizz Susan taking our upcoming deployment?" "Well, she doesn't like the fact that I'm leaving and all that, but she's putting up a stiff upper lip. Sometimes I think she's been crying, but I can't prove it. She quickly gets herself back to normal." "Yes suh, Mizz Lula's the same way. I can't ever prove it, but, sometimes I believe she cries herself to sleep 'cause we're about to leave." "Well, hopefully, we won't be gone long George, we'll whip those Yankee rascals real good, and be home for Christmas. That's what a lot of the men are saying, George, to their wives. However, I haven't said anything like that to Miss Susan, nor shall I 'cause its hearsay. Nobody knows how long we're gonna be up there 'cept the good Lord, and that's good 'cause I hope he's on our side.

As we rode up to the encampment, the sentry on picket duty saluted John Thomas, and said, "Good morning suh! The area is free of Yankee trash and vermin, all clear." "Thank you Sergeant, Carry on." "Yes suh!" "That was Sergeant Davis. He's one of our best noncommissioned officers in the outfit. When some of these young bucks starts talking about all the Yankees they're gonna kill, this and that, he gets in their face and says, "Well, now, soldier, that's good news. Why General Lee his own self is mighty proud to have soldiers like you in his Confederate Army. You just make sure that of all the soldiers that get killed, your momma and daddy ain't crying themselves to sleep every night 'cause one of 'em is YOU!"

This was the outer picket of the camp. John Thomas got to go home every night since he was the executive officer of Company C. The rest of the men, even the married ones had to sleep in the camp away from their families. This didn't bother the single men too much as they stayed up late playing cards, and drank home brewed beer, and told tales of how many Yankees they were gonna slaughter in their very first battle. The married soldiers didn't seem to mind too much outwardly. They'd all volunteered for this, and they were here because they wanted to be here. Although, after a while, their attitude became one of, "if we're going to fight, let's go instead of sitting here at home in the same county as our families and not be able to see 'em that much."

As we approached the second picket, he saluted John Thomas crisply, and said, "Good morning, suh. Nothing to report at this time." "Very well, carry on Corporal Dukes." "How long they gotta stay out here Mister John?" "They're only out here on post for 24 hours George. Corporal Duke's buddy Private Gatlin is asleep in his tent right now. Each of 'em is on post together for a

24 hour time period. They should be getting off in a few minutes since changeover is at 07:30. Colonel Gordon has decreed no soldier shall be on picket duty for more than 24 hours at a time. During the day, from 07:30 to 19:30 Captain McMillan ordered both sentry's awake.

After that, the senior man on Post decides who sleeps first. The smart ones make the junior man sleep first 'til 01:30, then they go to bed, and get a decent night's sleep, while the junior man is well rested when he goes on Post. But, by the time it's over, they're usually dragging, especially since it's so quiet and peaceful out here. Colonel Gordon knows there's no Yankee force within hundreds of miles from here, he's mainly ordered pickets set up to get the men in the mind set for war. When we set up camp, George, we have a 3 tiered Picket system. The first pickets are up to a mile from base camp. That way, if we're about to be attacked by the Yankees, it gives one or more of the pickets time pass the word to the second picket, who will in turn notify the third picket we're under attack by the Yankees, who will then notify the Officer of the Day.

"That's quite a system you got there Mister John. I reckon King David hisself mighta employed a system such as that to protect his brigands." "Yeah, George,

I reckon armies since the beginning of time have used this three tiered ring of protection strategy before. What it does is it protects the King, or the General, or just the troops themselves from being attacked while they're sleeping or even in the middle of the day. The men usually have picket duty no more than one or two days a week, and they don't mind right now 'cause they ain't being shot at. However, we'll see how they do once we get up to Virginia. Reckon they'll do just fine though. As we neared the third and final picket Private Hand saluted John Thomas and said, "Morning suh. All clear suh, nothing to report at this time." "Thank you, Private Hand," said John Thomas, and he returned his salute.

"Mister John, how come all those Gentlemen salute you every time they see you?" "Well, George I reckon it's a tradition going back all the way to the knights in England. What I hear is that when Knights were passing each other they would raise up their swords to each other in the form of a salute. It's sort of a greeting among warriors. Nowadays I reckon it has evolved a little to where enlisted troops salute officers, and officers of lesser rank like myself salute ones of a higher pay grade than theirs. George, to be honest with you, some days I salute so ma that I feel like my arm's gonna fall off. The good news is I'm telling all my men in "C" Company that when we get into the fight if they salute me I'm a gonna shoot 'em." Mister John chuckled at that, and so I asked him, "Why would you tell 'em that?" "Why??? 'Cause I don't wanta get shot when they salute me. You see, George, officers are the leaders of the army, and the Yankees know that if they can kill the officers first, it's like cutting the head off a snake. Once you do that, all the troops are gonna scatter, and they'll have no one to lead them. *That's why* I don't want 'em to salute me in the field when we go to war. See how I did that?" "Oh yeah. Yes suh. See exactly what you mean, like say if some highway man come and shoot your Pop, then the highway man will think he's cut off the head, and he can take over the place." "Exactly George, that's indeed what I'm telling you. Although, if what you said did take place, that highway man would have to deal with me and my brothers who'd be madder than wet hornets! But, I'm glad you understand. In fact, would you be so kind as to warn soldiers in the field not to salute me when we get to the war?" "I'd be happy to Mister John, you know that. Besides, your Pop would be right upset with me if you got shot and killed 'cause I didn't stop one of your men from saluting you."

"Yeah, I reckon he would be rightly upset, but it wouldn't be your fault 'cause these men know that I do not want to be saluted when we go to war. It really chaps my hide that the Army wants all the officers to be saluted, and don't they know that's the first thing a sniper will be looking for? When we get up to ole Virginny I'm gonna take some shoe polish and apply it to my lieutenant bars so somebody who doesn't know me won't know I'm an officer until when I get up close to 'em."

When we got there the men were eating their breakfast, and drinking their coffee. They asked us if we wanted any, but we politely declined.

After that, Mister John saluted Captain McMillan, and said, "Good morning, suh." Captain McMillan returned it, and said, "Good morning to you, suh. Care to join me in my office for a cup of coffee?" "Yes suh, don't mind if I do. George, you want to wait out here, I shouldn't be long." "Yes suh, I'll wait out here for you." Mister John went into Captain McMillan's office, and Captain McMillan said, "Take a seat, John. You want any cream for your coffee, or something stronger by chance?" John snickered and replied, "No suh, I believe I'm okay at the moment, but thank you for the offer." "My pleasure, suh, how's Mrs. Susan doing this morning?" "She's fine, but I reckon she's worried about the war and all. Still though she's putting on a stiff upper lip as our English cousins might say. How's your wife holding up in all this?" "She's taking it day by day. I guess she's just glad for the time we still have together until we have to depart for the war. I can tell she's not happy about me leaving, but, she knows the Yankees have to pay for what they're trying to do to us, affecting our way of life when we've never done a thing to them! Lord have mercy, have you seen some of the stuff those abolitionists are saying up North? It tears me up and gets me so angry. Why I'll bet you 99% of 'em troublemakers have never once set foot below the Mason-Dixon Line. So, who knows what will happen in the war, but I'm so proud of the state of Georgia and her patriotism. They asked for 12,000 volunteers, and 18,000 men showed up! I declare, if our neighbors to the east and to the west can supply those kind of numbers, I do believe we might be able to give the Yankees a run for their money. Don't tell the men I said this, but I do believe that even if we don't win, we'll make 'em think we did."

"It looks like we're gonna be leaving here pretty soon, John, I'm really not sure when exactly. After the South Carolinians drove the Yankees out of Fort Sumter, things are really starting to heat up North in Washington.

Lincoln is mobilizing as many soldiers as he can, as fast as he can, same as we are, and higher command is speculating that since it's the end of May 1861 right now, we may be deploying our forces in a fortnight or so. So let Mrs. Susan be aware of this, as well as your dear Mama and Pop, so they'll have full knowledge of our timeframe. Also please tell George to tell Lula as well. Lawd knows the whole county knows when Miss Lula's upset. "Captain McMillan and John Thomas both snickered at that. They'd both been around Lula first hand when she told a field hand off or popped one of our children when they got out of line, They were glad that they had the full respect and admiration of my Lula, for heaven knows, indeed, half the state of Georgia knows how she is when she gets her dander up.

"Captain McMillan, I'm gonna show George around the camp, and introduce him to some of the folks since he's going with us and all if you don't mind, suh?" "Yes suh, by all means take him around and introduce him to some of the men. In fact, I'm quite envious of you John Thomas for being able to take your own servant with you off to war and all, for my family doesn't have any servants like that." "Well, thank you, Captain I'll have George look after you as well while we're up North. He'll be happy to do it since he's also known you your whole life since your family moved here from South Carolina." "Thank you, suh, mighty kind of you, John Thomas, mighty kind of you, suh." "Well, thank you, suh, it's nothing really, and we're all in this together to teach the Yankees to stay out of our affairs, as we stay out of theirs."

Mister John stepped out of the Captains office and walked over to me. He had a pleased look over his face and asked me if they gave me any breakfast. "Yes suh, they ended up practically begging me to take some breakfast, so I did. Woo wee, boy was it good! I've been hearing about how great the food y'all soldiers is eating out here, and everything I heard was right, and then some!

"Yeah, George, it's definitely delicious and all, but nothing beats being able to sit at home with your wife and kids every day and night where you belong. Although, the really young men, and the young boys are having a blast out here! Telling lies all night, smoking their pipes, and drinking out of their swoon bottles. That was Private Jones who served you your breakfast. He's one of the funniest boys of Company C. The other day when we were out test firing our rifles he had those troopers laughing so hard they were crying out of both eyes! Let's get our horses, George, and then I'll show you the rest of the camp." "Yes suh, I'd enjoy that." Mister John and I galloped down a small dirt path crowded with oak and pine trees lining both sides of the worn out path. After about a half mile down this narrow path, all of a sudden the wall of trees ended, and it opened up onto a beautiful field with at least 50 tents spread out all over the field lined up perfectly in what looked like 5 rows of 10 tents, each tent lining up perfectly with the one in front of it, beside it, and behind it. "George, out here is base camp. This is smack dab in the middle of the area where we train. It's nice and pretty out here at night. You can see all the stars, and when there's a harvest moon out, it almost feels like you can see just as far as you can see right now with the morning sun up. Behind that last tent over yonder on your right are the stables where all the horses are kept, and over that ridge yonder on my left is the field where the men test fire their rifles and practice how they're gonna do squad rushes against the Yankees. Two weeks ago we had a harvest moon, and we were out there shooting, practicing squad rushes, and bayonet fighting 'till 2 a.m. It was a hoot" Mister John steered his horse in that general direction, and I followed a little bit behind his. I was glad to be out here this morning and get to see firsthand what everybody in the county had been talking about all spring, the mobilization of Company C, the "Davis Rifles." Word is that Mr. Johnson donated this part of his plantation for the men to train on for the duration of the war.

Everybody in the county was starting to step up and made contributions to the war effort in the South. Why, Mister Carson told me recently that the entire South had placed an embargo on its cotton to show how valuable a commodity it is. But that set me to thinking, "Why in the world would we put an *embargo on our richest crop?*" Lawd if that don't make no sense to me at all. Reckon folks smarter than me can figure that one out. Instead I hear the planters in Macon County are now going to replace all their cotton fields with vegetables instead for the duration of the war. Ladies are helping sew uniform items for their husbands, and those gentlemen who are too old to fight are doing whatever they can to support the troops instead.

Soon all those newly planted vegetable fields will feed not only the South, but the Confederate Army as well. Mister Carson told me that Napoleon said "An army marches on its stomach." The more I thought about it, I reckon little old Napoleon was right. As we crossed the ridge we saw about 50 young soldiers all up on the firing line making their rifles ready to fire. "Shooters, ready on the right, ready on left, you may fire when your targets appear. *TARGETS!!!*" A deafening explosion occurred, and I wish I had brought some balls of cotton to quickly stuff into my ears, 'cause for the next 5 minutes my ears were ringing like a church bell inside my head at high noon on Sunday. Mister Carson and I rode our mounts right up to the back of the line and Mister John half shouted, "Great shooting, boys! This here is my servant, and *friend* George. He's going with us to Ole Virginny, so y'all give him a warm welcome from the Davis Rifles!" "Glad you're coming with us George!" Someone shouted. "Glad to have you, George," a young boy no more than 18 (if that) shouted. A few more nice greetings like this, and I was truly touched by their gentleness and their kindnesses towards me. Gently, I tipped my hat towards them and said, "Thank you, gentlemen. It's good to be here with y'all.

Let me know if you ever need anything." With that, the sergeant running the firing line told the shooters. "All right, you knuckleheads, get yo sorry hides down theah, and check and see if any of y'all hit the target." When the "knuckleheads" made their way to each target I heard, "Yippee, lookee here, Elijah, mine hit BULLS EYE, DEAD CENTER! How'd you shoot?" I heard one of 'em say. Elijah responded, "Pretty good, Benjamin, not quite good as you. Reckon mine missed dead center by the size of a pin head." "Sho nuff did! 'Em Yankees won't know what hit 'em."

I was impressed with these boys marksmanship, but after thinking about it I realized I shouldn't be. Most of 'em had been shooting practically their whole lives since they was knee high to a duck. 'Course I had done the same thing practically with John Thomas and his 3 brothers, and they could all shoot just as good as these soldiers, or *better*. "Well, George, that's pretty much it of the camp," Mister John said as we turned our horses around and headed back the way we'd come. "George, Captain McMillan said he believes we'll be getting orders for Virginia in about 2 weeks. Could you go back and tell Lula that, as well as Pop?" "Yes suh, I'd be happy to. You don't need me to stay out here and help you today?" "Naw, George, but I sure do appreciate the offer." With that we rode in silence and enjoyed the pretty countryside of Marshallville on the south side of our county. When we reached the outer picket, he said, "Thanks for coming out here this morning with me, George, to meet the men. They enjoyed meeting you, and I do believe you'll be a wonderful addition to the Company." "Thank you. suh, when I get back I'll be sure to let Mister Carson know we expect to be leaving in about 2 or 3 weeks." "Thank you, George, you're most kind." "Yes suh, my pleasure." I watched the soldier at the gate salute John Thomas, and then I headed back home.

"Oh Lawd, God of heaven and earth, be with these fine young man and keep 'em safe and sound. Lawd they believe they're doing your will, and I don't know if they are or aren't dear Lawd. In the meantime help us to trust in you, and you alone.

Thank you so much for all thy many blessings you've given the Carson family, Father, and may we be able to share your blessings with others, as you've so richly blessed us, in Jesus' mighty and majestic name, Amen." That was the prayer I prayed on the way back to Carson House. Didn't know what I was feeling right now, but it looks like we're definitely going to war now with the North, no holding back now. The word was that lots of outfits like Mister John's were already in Virginia, and obviously a whole lot more were on the way. These men weren't drafted, they *volunteered. All of 'em!* They feel their whole way of life is under assault, and they're happily marching off to war to defend it. Wonder if it's like that up North? I wonder if some farm boys up North who don't own slaves are willing to die so these boys here from Macon County *can't?*

This is gonna upset Mister and Mizz Carson something fierce, but, they knew if wasn't far off. This is the result of at least 30 years of arguments between North and South over slavery, and now we've done it. Those boys I just saw shooting like Davey Crockett are most likely gonna be casualties of the war themselves if they make it, and what's gonna happen to the families of the ones who don't? Lawd have mercy! Land sakes alive, why can't those uppity Yankees just leave the South alone. The South ain't done nothing to 'em. Heaven's sake, there's probably always been slavery, and probably always will be. Didn't the Lawd say, "For ye have the poor always with you; but me ye have not always?" I reckon you could say the same about slavery, though I'm not a fortune teller. Speaking of the poor, we aren't poor! I can honestly say that I don't remember the last time I was ever truly hungry, especially with Lula's cooking. But if a man can't even remember the last time he *might* have been hungry, owns his own home outright, and has his own land such as I do, I don't exactly see the problem. Reckon Lula and I got it better off than half the North.

No need to worry longer on this topic, for its giving me an awful headache that isn't good for an old man.

Used to think I'm still a young man, and I am in my mind, but my body sometimes tells me I ain't. Mister Carson just turned 59 years old, and I've always thought we were about the same age since I've known him almost my whole life. Anyway, it feels good just to be able to get up every day and do the things I used to do when I was half my age but not have to worry about doing 'em if I don't want to.

As I got back to Carson House, Lula was on the front porch, so she yelled, "Hey honey! How you be?" "Hello, Sweetie, just fine. The soldiers all can shoot a gnat's eye from 100 yards!" "Dat's good 'cause most of 'em been shooting since dey be knee high to a duck." "Yes ma'am, you're right about that! Is Mister Carson at home?" "Yeah Honey, he in his library. Want me to tell him you heah?" "No thank you, Honey, I'll just go see him." "Okay den."

When I entered the library Mister Carson was sitting in his favorite chair smoking his pipe. Eyes closed, seemingly at peace with the world. "Morning, George." "Oh, good morning, suh. I didn't realize you heard me come in?" "Heard ya talking outside to the best cook in the South!" He chuckled a little, and so did I. "Please have a seat, George. Tell me how Company C is getting along." "Well suh, I reckon you heard me tell Lula they can all shoot a gnat in the eye from a 100 yards." "As they should be able to, all those boys have been shooting since they were knee high to a duck." I chuckled, apparently everybody around here thinks on the same level as everyone else. Anyway, he continued, "George, did you find out when they're leaving for Virginia?" "Not exactly, suh, however, that's why I came to see you. Mister John told me to tell you and Mizz Carson that Captain McMillan expects the Company to get orders for Virginia in about two weeks, though they haven't heard anything official as of yet." Mister Carson puffed on his pipe a bit, and closed his eyes again. Lawd have mercy, that Virginia tobacco sure smelled good! The doctor told me once that your sense of smell is one of the strongest senses. He told me that dogs as a matter of fact can smell seven times stronger than a gentleman. Anyway, I say that 'cause it reminded me of the first time I ever smelled Virginia tobacco.

Must've been about 5 or 6 at the time, but will never forget that almost magical smell! "George, do you have your pipe with you?" "Yes suh." "Well fire it up my friend." "Suh, I reckon I better hold off on that incase Lula should see me. She says I smoke way too much, but thank you for your kind offer." Mister Carson chuckled at that. "I'm sorry to hear that, George. Whenever Mrs. Martha gets to squawking about my smoking, I just take the dog for a walk in the field. By the time I get back she's forgot about my pipe, and if she's still not in a good humor, she's bellyaching about something else." The doctor told me once that smoking a pipe is good for a man's health. He would have known, he lived to be 101 years young over in Crawford County. I expect he told me that over 40 years ago when I first took up my pipe, and I've never looked back since.

"You know what, George? That's exactly the problem that has beset our country. Everybody's worried about everybody else's business. The Yankees are worried about our business, and everybody's worried about everybody else's health. Why can't folks just worry about themselves? The Yankees are threatening to take my 4 boys from me George. Robert's talking again about this blasted war to come, and how "glorious it's going to be for our nation of the confederacy." It nearly tore his mother's heart out. She's a regal lady George, but she's quite upset over the prospects of losing her four boys to the Yankees, and can't say as I blame her. Hopefully, if it comes to an all out, war George, it will be over quickly, for I fear a protracted war like the Revolution will decimate us." "Yes suh, hopefully the South can whip them Yankees back above the Mason-Dixon Line, and they'll leave our business to *us.*" "Hopefully, George, hopefully they don't take this old man's head to the grave in grief and sadness." "Yes suh, that would be awful. Suh, I was reading my Bible this morning in the book of Jeremiah, in the 29th chapter in verse 11 he said, "For I know the thoughts I think toward you, saith the Lawd, thoughts of peace, and not of evil, to give you an unexpected end. Then ye shall call upon me, and ye shall go and pray unto me, and I will hearken unto you. And ye shall seek me, and find me, when ye shall search for me with all your heart." "That's a good passage, George.

Jeremiah was speaking to the sons of Israel who had lost their way with the God of Israel, and turned to Baal, that ancient god of the devil. Jeremiah was reminding the ancient Israelites to come back to the true God, not one of stone, and metal. If only our nation would turn back to the God of Israel, will we truly be saved." Mister Carson pointed at me with his pipe, and said, "You know, George, first time I ever read that I believed he was talking just to the ancient Hebrews, but the more times I read it, I believe he's talking to *us as well.*

"Which leads me to believe that the Yankees and the South must put their trust in the God of Israel, or we will face a disaster to our nation that will take generations to be overcome. Anyhow, George, Mister Robert wants to go to town in Reynolds this morning. Would you mind going with him to see that he stays out of trouble and doesn't disgrace the family name?" "Yes suh, I'd be happy to. Where does he want to go?" "I believe he said he wanted to go to the general store. I'll send him over to your house, and then y'all can depart unto town." "Should we take the wagon, or ride our horses suh?" "Ugh, I reckon you ought to take the wagon, 'cause if y'all ride your horses, he's gonna want to race, and last time he went to town on my favorite horse he nearly broke the poor stallion's leg for racing it, and I tore his hide so bad, he had to sit on a pillow at school for a month. All the boys and girls made fun of him for it, and he always got red in the face over it, and rightly he should have! That boy's gotta learn that he can't just get up and go do whatever he wants, whenever he wants." "Yes suh, he's a teenager, full of spunk and vinegar." "I know it George, but when you get as old as we are, it's a lot tougher to raise a teenage boy than it is when you're John Thomas' age." "Yes suh, luckily all my children grew up a long time ago, or I'd be facing the same trouble you are with Mister Robert." Mister Carson chuckled, "he's a good boy George, you know he is. He's just a little rascal, and at our age we should be able to relax, and enjoy life. Not constantly be worried about what stunt my teenage boy has pulled next." "Yes suh, I'll get the wagon hitched up, and wait outside for Mister Robert." "Thank you, George, I sure do appreciate it!" "My pleasure, suh."

I passed Lula on the porch, and she called out to me, "George, baby where you going?" "Honey, Mister

Carson asked me to take Mister Robert into Reynolds, said he wanted to go to the drugstore." "You going to de general store? What he want at de general store?" "There's no telling baby." "Mister Carson just wanted me to go with him to make sure he didn't get into any devilment. We'll be back before dinner. Is there anything that the Carson's need, or that we need for the house, Honey?" "Naw, we gots most everthang all of us need right now. All right den, you take care Mista Robert ya heah George?" "Yes ma'am, I will." By the time I had the wagon all hitched up and in front of the house Mister Robert came bounding out the front door. "Hey George, you ready to go to Reynolds?" "Yes suh, Mister Robert, what you need so bad that we go to go to town for?" "Ah nothing really, just wanted to get out of the house. Reckon I'm getting cabin fever since school let out, and there ain't much to do." "All right, well let's get along. I told Lula we'd be back for dinner." "Sounds good George, let's go." With that he jumped in the wagon, and we were off. The horse was taking us at a casual trot up River Road a few miles to the highway. "There's the Gordon plantation, George. Everybody's saying General Lee might make Mister Gordon a General! Wouldn't that be something?" "Yeah, that'd be mighty fine Mister

Robert. Hopefully this blasted war will be over quickly and the Yankees don't take everything we've worked hard for over the years from us." Robert didn't say anything to that, just rode along in silence. Now that we were out of sight of the Carson House, *and LULA,* I grabbed my pipe and lit it. Puffing in silence, hoping to get these gnats out of my face, and give me some relief from all this talk of war. Don't nobody know that nothing good comes from a war, and nobody wins? Why the war ain't even started yet, and it's likely to give poor Mizz Carson a heart attack. Poor Mizz Martha, heaven has never seen a more kind and gentle soul. Mister Carson used to make her out like a dragon lady, but I ain't never seen anything like that in her.

We turned left on the highway to go into town only a few miles further down the road. If we would've turned right that would've taken us towards Fort Valley and Macon. However, our direction was westward bound. If you went past Reynolds, you could be in Columbus, Georgia in about half a day in a wagon. I ain't never been to Columbus, but they say it's a pretty little town. It sits in the county of Muscogee. Mister Carson told me that's the name of an Indian tribe of Creek Indians that used to live in the area before the white men moved in. Now he says they live all the way out in Oklahoma. Reckon that wasn't too long ago that they left. I believe that was about 30 years ago when they were pushed out by Andrew Jackson and his forces.

I heard a man tell Mister Carson once that on the north side of this highway there isn't any gnats, and that they only live south of the highway. Lawd almighty, what I wouldn't give to live on the north side of that highway! A body can learn to manage around the gnats, though they sure are a nuisance though. When we arrived in town, Robert saw soldiers out of the field at the general store getting some supplies for their camp. He met one to whom he introduced himself, and the soldier called himself the Quartermaster. He said he was there at the bequest of Lieutenant Carson to get provisions for the men at the general feed & supply store. He was loading up 10 different wagons apiece. One wagon had 10 sacks of flour; another had 10 sacks of salt; and another had 10 sacks of sugar. The last wagon was full of tobacco, corn cob pipes, and cleaning supplies for pipes, & 25 sacks of yeast. Robert asked him what they needed all that yeast for, but the quartermaster said he didn't know. "Sergeant Tanner who runs our firing range told me if I got him 25 sacks of yeast for his platoon, he'd get me a chit to make sure I didn't have to ever go out and shoot. Since I wear glasses, and couldn't hit the broadside of a barn I got 'em for him." I was studying all the pipe supplies they had on their wagons. Mister Carson had all sorts of items such as these. Me, I didn't feel it worth fooling over, and mine smoked just fine.

As we pulled up to it I could see cases and cases of bottles filled with a brown colored liquid underneath all the tobacco. I reckon it was so none of the ladies could see it, and wondered what in tarnation those soldiers were actually doing out there at Marshallville. Robert informed the Quartermaster Private Westberry that Lieutenant Carson was his oldest brother. He said, "Our executive officer. He's a real fine gentleman!" "That's my brother, suh!" "Well, ain't that something. I'll be sure and let him know we saw you in town and tell him hello. My name is Private Westberry, I'm the Quartermaster. Make sure the troopers are good and taken care of with food, uniforms, and other knickknacks." "That's mighty fine suh, I sure wish I could be out there with y'all, but my daddy won't let me enlist 'til I'm 18. Land sakes alive!!! By then the war'll be good and over, and I'll still be stuck down here on the farm while y'all are having all the fun up North killing Yankees!" Private Westberry finally noticed me and said, "Hey there George! We met this morning at the firing range. Well we didn't actually meet, but I said hey to you along with everybody else when Lt. Carson introduced you. Good to see you again, I'm sure we'll see you soon enough with us departing soon and all." "WHAT!!! Y'all are leaving soon? I can't believe it! I didn't expect y'all to leave until the fall," Robert lamented. "Well, scuttlebutt is saying it could be 2 or 3 weeks, but no more than that," said Private Westberry. Robert was privately furious that he couldn't be out there training with them for war, and now they were actually about to leave. It wasn't fair! Why did everybody else get to go and kill Yankees but him? Inwardly he swore to himself that if there was any way, any way at all, he was gonna go be with his brother and kill Yankees if it was the last thing he ever did!

"Well, it sure was nice meeting you, but we've got to get back to Marshallville so the men'll have something to eat for dinner. Good to see you again George." "Good to see you again, suh. Y'all be careful out there." "We'll do it!" With that, the Quartermaster and the rest of his minions headed back to Marshallville and the hungry troops.

Chapter 4

I headed the wagon over to the general store so Mister Robert could see whatever it was that he just had to see. Before I had even stopped the wagon, Robert was out of the wagon, and hustling up the steps of the general store. After I parked the wagon, I sat and waited a bit for Mister Robert. Lawd, how he talks! Too bad that child can't see that he's the luckiest boy in his family right now? All his older brothers feel obliged to go to war to defend their honor, but Robert, he has an excuse not to go off and get his self killed, and he don't even care. He's so bull headed, won't listen to nobody about it. "Dear Lawd, please let this war be over by the time that stubborn boy is old enough to go and fight. Please don't take Mister Carson's head down to grave in sadness. Thank you, Lawd, Amen."

After a while Robert came running down the steps, faster than he'd gone up 'em. "Ready to go George?" "Yes suh, I am. What you got in that sack young man?" "Candy, you want some?" "No, thank you. Now don't you be eating all that candy at once or you'll rot your teeth out. You hear me?" "Yes, George, I promise." As we headed back to the Carson House we rode in blissful silence. It was a gorgeous day, not a cloud in the sky! Never been anywhere but Georgia my whole life, and I reckon that's all right, 'cause everywhere you go people are nice as they can be. The scenery is always pleasant to the eye, whether it's the flat plains filled withcotton fields, or the Piedmont region, and its rolling hills as you go on towards Atlanta. This is my home, and this is where I belong. Atlanta's real nice, same as Macon, but at the end of the day what a man needs is land. Land to look over as the sun sets in its beautiful hues of red, and orange, and land to look over in the morning as it rises, becoming its fullest around noon. Yes suh, there ain't no place better than the great state of Georgia!!!

After dinner, I asked Robert if he wanted to go fishing, but he declined. Lawd have mercy, I wonder what's gotten into that boy.

Must be feeling melancholy 'cause he can't go off and fight with the rest of his brothers. Later that night after supper I told Lula that we'd probably be leaving in about 2 or 3 weeks, and she thanked me for telling her and went straight to bed.

When Company C finally got orders, I was fishing with Robert in the Flint River on a Saturday afternoon. By the time we got back to the house, John Thomas was riding up on his horse at almost a full gallop. "George, George, We got our orders, We leave on Tuesday!" "Great! You go on and tell your folks, and I'll finish up packing." Robert looked like he was about to cry.

After a quick weekend of packing and feasting, the men of Company C told their wives and families good bye. I reckon it was easier on the single soldiers to say good bye than the married ones. Lula told me, "George, doan go getting yo self kilt by no Yankee, 'cause if you do they gone have to deal with likes of me! And take care 'dat boy Mista John, ya heah?" "Yes ma'am! We'll be back here before you know it."

Captain McMillan had let all the men, officers and enlisted off for the weekend for one last chance to be with their families. For many of these young lads, unbeknownst to 'em, this would be the last time they would ever see each other, but luckily they didn't know it, otherwise it would've been a very sad goodbye I'm sure.

Years ago, somebody told me that there were around 139 men that left with Company C on Tuesday, June 18th, 1861. While roughly 61 of those men would never come home. What a travesty. If only the two sides could've found a way to avoid this calamity, much grief could've been spared. But this was not to be. Looking back upon the war, I reckon it was an unavoidable train wreck in the making from the start of this nation until the Battle of Fort Sumter, when it became inevitable that war was coming.

Our Company C made its way to Augusta, GA, and then finally made our destination at Richmond, VA two days later. Everyone was excited to be here. Even Mister John was most excited as I was, since neither one of us had ever been out of the state of Georgia before. While Montgomery, Al, was the first capital of the South, soon after the attack on Fort Sumter, Richmond, VA., became the new capital. Situated on the banks of the James River, Richmond was chosen as the new capital because of Virginia's strategic importance to the war effort.

About a week later, on Wednesday June 26th, 1861, Company C was mustered into the 12th Georgia Regiment in the Capital Square at Richmond. Colonel Johnson of Virginia was the commanding officer for the regiment, and had the men billeted just outside the city limits. Richmond was a real nice town, and everybody was real friendly and happy to help the soldiers in any way they thought they might be able to.

Chapter 5

John Thomas was taken in by a friendly old widow named Mrs. Clara Jones Dooley, a kindly old lady, who said she was born on the very day that Thomas Jefferson wrote the Declaration of Independence. She didn't look that old to me. In fact, she didn't look any older than I was, and I was young enough to be her son. She had a soft voice, with a rich southern accent, and an easy going smile to set you at ease. She had a huge manor house and a heap of servants. "Now, George, you don't worry about a thing, Honey, while you're here. Just see that John Thomas is taken care of, and you may have your run of the place," she told me when we got there, and she smiled that pretty smile, with those pretty blue eyes that seemed to hold both sweetness, and mischief behind them at once.

Don't recall how long we stayed with Mrs. Dooley, but as long as we were there, she expected her guests to be treated like kings, and treated like kings we were indeed. One of the things Mrs. Dooley liked to do at night was to hear John Thomas tell her about his family back in Georgia. She'd sit and listen for hours as he told her about Macon County, and his family, and everything in between. Her family had landed in Virginia in 1761, and her father had been a planter before he joined Colonel George Washington's Army at the start of the Revolutionary War. She said after the war he didn't like to talk much about it, except every now and then when he was deep into his cups at night, and she would sneak up on him and ask him questions about the war.

At first she said he would get real angry with her, for he knew what she up to but after that, when he was deep into his cups he would talk about the war.

He told her how 3 of his brothers were killed by the British, and how they burned down his farm in the middle of the war, leaving his wife and children to fend for themselves in the countryside in the middle of a brutally cold winter. "War is horrible, Clara! Don't you ever forget that! Nothing good comes out of it, and nobody wins. The consequences of war are hit hardest on the families of soldiers who have to bear the costs of the loss of their loved ones. Worse yet, Clara, is when their loved ones come home missing arms and legs and being badly mangled and handicapped for life by the Redcoats."

I reckon if we'd stayed there the entire war, she could've told us a new, and exciting story every single night. Many years later I heard through the grapevine that the Yankees burned down her house for harboring rebel soldiers there during the war. Such a shame, for that was the finest house I have ever seen in my lifetime. It had marble floors, a curving staircase in front of the front door that curved on both sides of the house. Not only did it have a beautiful front porch that wrapped around the entire house, but upstairs there was a balcony that had a view of the city that took one's breath away, for you could see the entire city from it! Lawd I do hope indeed that she was with you in glory when the Yankees burned that house, for there's never been another one like it!

'Course *nobody* can hold a candle to Lula's cooking, but the food Mrs. Dooley's cooks prepared for us was enough to make John Thomas and me not forget Lula's cooking, but to be able to not remember it while we enjoyed Mrs. Dooley's kitchen very much so. John Thomas took his meals in the dining room with the other gentlemen and Mrs. Dooley. However, being the kind Christian lady that she was, Mrs. Dooley allowed me to take my victuals in her actual kitchen. She said she knew I was lonely, and homesick for my Lula the great cook (oh yes, I told her everything about her) and wanted to make sure that I was taken good care of as well.

I don't rightly recall how long we stayed with Mrs. Dooley, but I do remember it being a very pleasant time. Nobody was shooting at us, and we were in a fine home, taken in by a wonderful Christian lady who took splendid care of us.

Every now and then we got a letter from home telling how proud the Carsons were of us, as well as the good folks of Macon County. "Dear Lula, all is well up here in Richmond, VA. We're staying for now with a kind old Christian Lady, who lives in a mansion fit for a king I say! Hope you and the children now grown up are doing well, and John Thomas and I hope to be home for Christmas. All my love, your faithful husband of many years now...George." Mizz Carson was kind enough to write letters back to me for Lula, who couldn't write.

"Dear George, It was so good to hear from you, Honey. Glad you and Mister John are being well taken care of by Mrs. Dooley, and we all hope and pray that y'all may be able to stay the entire war with her, at her house, instead of going out and getting killed by some Yankee. All the Carsons are well, along with your lovely wife, children, and grandchildren. Keep Mr. John safe and yourself as well. Hopefully y'all are right, and you'll be home for Christmas. Your loving wife of many years…Lula.

It was almost a year I suspect before the 12th Georgia Regiment was able to get their teeth cut real good in the war. In between this time we had been comfortably provided for by Mrs. Dooley and her servants. Whatever we wanted, if she had it we got it. After a quiet winter, Mister John and his men were told to march towards McDowell, Virginia. Most of the way there we took the train, but, after Staunton, we had to get out and march on foot. Somebody said it was about 33 miles from there to McDowell, so once the company was formed up, we split up in a column of two's, and started marching towards McDowell.

It was about 7 o'clock in the morning when we started marching, and it wasn't until about 10 o'clock at night when we finally arrived at the base camp to reinforce the rest of the regiment. A few days after that, in a hotly contested battle, the Davis Rifles' commanding officer Captain McMillan was killed while fighting the Yankees in his first and last battle ever.

Not only did the Yankees kill Captain McMillan, but they also killed 3 other Captains, 4 Lieutenants, and they also killed or wounded 250 noncommissioned officers of the 12th Georgia Regiment. Just last week, Mister John's younger brother James had enlisted in the Davis Rifles at Marshallville. His sweet wife Melissa Bryan Carson and his parents gave him a hug and a kiss, bid him good luck, and said they'd be praying for him and his older brother often.

When James got off the train in Richmond, I gave him a big hug, and said, "Mister James, look at you in your uniform! Why I declare if you don't look even more handsome than your older brother!" "Thanks, George, how's he doing up here?" "Why he's doing fine son, he's doing fine. All we've been doing up here for the last year is receiving lots of gifts, and ministrations from the sweet hearted ladies of Richmond. They're Heaven's gift to the South! They consider it an honor to keep up the lonely soldiers spirits and feed 'em hefty amounts of victuals." "Sounds great, George, I heard a rumor on the train that Company C is leaving soon for McDowell to fight the Yankees. You reckon it's true?" "Yes suh, it is indeed. The company's leaving in the morning, so you showed up just in time!" "Great! I'm glad I didn't miss my chance to fight the Yankees." With that, I loaded up Mister James's trunk in the back of the wagon, and we were off to Mrs. Dooley's house. Mrs. Dooley saw us pull up before the Manor House, and came walking down the steps to greet Mister James.

"Why I declare, you must be James, John Thomas' little brother! I saw the resemblance as soon as I saw y'all coming up the drive. I'm Mrs. Clara Jones Dooley, and it's so good to know you. George would you kindly get Mister James' things, and put them in the bedroom we made up for him?" "Yes ma'am, be happy to do it." "Thank you. Come on James, I'll take you to your brother. I know he'll be so happy to see you.

Mrs. Dooley took James' arm in one of hers and walked up the front porch steps and led him into the house. "Mrs. Dooley, ma'am, umm, this is without a doubt the finest home I have ever seen." "Why thank you, James. Would believe I've lived here for 50 years?

This is the house my dearly beloved husband had built for me many years ago. Bless his soul he was such a fine Christian man, always kind to orphans and widows. The good Lord took him way too young 15 years ago. During the Mexican-American War he contracted malaria in Chapultepec. The Marine Corps shipped his body back home." Mrs. Dooley looked as if she was about to faint, but Mister James stepped in quietly and said, "I'm so sorry for your loss ma'am. He must've been a fine man. I've studied that battle and understand a whole lot of folks died in it." "Bless you. Thank you for your concern." With that she brightened up and went to find Mister John.

Opening the door up to the parlor she announced, "Mr. John, you have company." Mister John and other officers were playing poker. With cigars in everyone's mouth, the room was filled with so much smoke it looked as if a train's smokestack had blown in through the window.

Mister John had his back to the door, and when he set his hand down and turned around his cigar almost fell out of his mouth. When James started to salute his executive officer, Mister John ran over and bear hugged him. "James, what are you doing here?

Look at you in your uniform! Don't you look spiffy, when did you enlist?" "Last Thursday on the 1st, they allowed me to spend the weekend with Melissa and the family, then on Monday morning they sent me up here."

"That's outstanding, James, because we've sitting up here for almost a year being treated like Kings, and then you show up and ruin it for us, 'cause we just got word we're leaving in the morning for battle." "So it is true? I heard a rumor on the train, and in Richmond." "Yes suh, indeed it is true. We've got to be formed up at the train station tomorrow at 0400, which means we'll have to leave here no later than 0300." "Well, I guess we'll have to go to bed early tonight I reckon then." "Yeah, but not before we catch up on everybody back home, we're about to eat supper, why don't you go get your room all settled, and freshen up, and then we'll have some supper. How's that sound?" With that, James popped to attention and stiffly saluted his older brother. Mister John brought his arm up to his head in a vague impression of returning the salute, and James replied, "Suh, on the double, right away, Suh!" John Thomas chuckled and said, "Look knucklehead, when we're in front of the troops, and other officers' act that way, but when it's just me and you, my name is John, and yours is James." James thought about that for half a second, then quickly replied in a loud, crisp voice, *"YES S…I mean John."* John smiled then said, "Good. See ya in a little bit."

After supper they retreated to Mrs. Dooley's wide front porch and took in the view of Richmond, and the sun getting lower and lower in the sky. James pulled out his pipe, and John Thomas pulled out a cigar he'd won in the poker game. "I hear these things come up here from Cuba. They're the best cigars you ever saw." "You got an extra one by chance?"

Mister John smiled at his brother and said, "I reckon I might have an extra one in my room. George, would you be so kind as to get me my swoon bottle and three glasses please?" "Why yes suh, my pleasure." While I went to get Mister John's request, I wondered how Lula and the Carsons were doing. Coming back outside, Mister John said, "George, you got your pipe on you?" "Yes suh, I do." "Good, pull up a chair, and would you please pour each of us a glass before you do that?" "Yes, suh." "Thank you, George. Gentlemen, I'd like to propose a toast to the Carson family. May we be strong, may we keep our honor, and may we be faithful to our cause," with that we all clinked glasses with each other, and settled back in our rockers.

As we all took a sip, that first one felt warm when it entered my stomach and gave me a nice feeling. I chuckled inside as I remembered Mister Carson years ago telling me to sip it, not chug it.

James and I lit our pipes, while John Thomas lit his cigar. Mister John told us our pipes smelled good, and we told him that his cigar did as well. As we gazed down upon the city of Richmond, with the red sun setting over top of it I realized that this wonderful moment of peace, and reunion would be short lived. In less than 12 hours we'd all be boarding the train and heading out west.

"So brother, how's the family back home? How's mother & Pop?" "Pop is fine; mother looks tired all the time; and she frequently naps. Susan and the children are fine, and everything else is pretty much the same. You know home, it does not hardly ever change." "Ain't it the truth?" "Yes, indeed, and George, Miss Lula is fine, and she asked me to give you this." "Thank you Mister James, what is it?" Mister James reached into his coat, and pulled out an envelope which said on the front in almost illegible handwriting, since my lovely wife Lula wrote my name.

Mister George Carson

My Dear George,

Hope you are doing well Honey. Miss Carson was so nice to write you this letter for me. She says one day when she isn't so tired she will teach me how to read & write. I miss you Baby, and pray for you first thing in the morning and last thing at night. Try to be safe, Honey, and take great care of Mister John.

Your loving wife of many years,
Lula

"So how's Miss Lula getting along, George?" "She's fine suh, says she's praying for me, and that your mother plans on teaching her how to read & write when she's not so tired." Then Mister James said, "I reckon the stress of the war is wearing her out. Doctor said she needs to rest, so that's what she does. And to think her and Pop have been worried sick about y'all for a year now, and low and behold, y'all have been living the good life up here in Richmond like y'all were kings or something."

Mister John smiled a sheepish smile, took a snip, and a couple of puffs of his cigar, and said, "Brother, whenever our country asks us to sacrifice for it, George and I will gladly sacrifice ourselves for it. And if our great nation chooses for us to suffer here under the care of Mrs. Dooley, then so be it, anything for the cause." Mister James and I let out belly ripping laughs for a long time, until finally Mister John had to break up the joking. "In all seriousness gentlemen, I do believe the fun stops tomorrow, and perhaps all the extra attention the proud ladies of Richmond have been happy to provide us over the course of time will disappear.

We'll be forced to endure more rustic conditions like the rest of the Army. Oh, I almost forgot how are Joe and Robert getting along?"

"Joe's doing fine, and he's with I Company, 4th Georgia Infantry. Robert's his normal rambunctious self. Lord how he talks about running off and signing up to be in Company C so he can be with his two older brothers! He's about to drive Ma & Pop half nuts! Hopefully the war'll be over before he's old enough to enlist." "Yes suh, I reckon we were all high strung like he is when we were 16, in 20 years when he's my age, he'll soon realize that young men often can't see the forest for the trees like we couldn't when we were 16. All we cared about were the pretty young ladies in our Sunday School Class. That's all. He'll grow up eventually as well," said Mister John.

Chapter 6

About a month after the Yankees slaughtered us at McDowell, VA, Mister John got a telegram from his father Mister Carson explaining that his Mother had passed away in her sleep. *"My dear John Thomas, it is with deep regret I inform you of the passing away of your mother in her sleep last night. She never felt any pain in her passing from this earth. She had been bedridden for months now, and now she resides in Providence. Please make her proud son, you and your brothers are all I have left now. Your Proud Father, J.J. Carson."* After he read the telegraph silently three different times he handed it to his brother James. When Mister James had finished reading it he handed it to me. Lawd have mercy! Mister Carson and Lula must be tore up right now! How they both loved that woman, for she was the rock behind Mister Carson that gave him the strength he needed to be as successful a planter as he was, and now Mizz Carson's gone forever. The Lawd giveth, and the Lawd taketh away. BLESSED BE THE NAME OF THE LAWD.

Sometime that summer, nobody ever really figured out where Mister James was wounded at, or in which battle, but he contracted bilious fever.

At first it wasn't too bad on him, but by the end of the summer they had him in the hospital over in Lynchburg, VA where he said he was nauseous, throwing up literally everything that went into his stomach, and having to go to the outhouse all the time. That poor young man was in a miserable way, and then on a rainy Wednesday morning, August 27, 1862 Mister James threw up for the last time, closed his eyes, and never opened them again. Mister James left behind his wife of 6 years, Mizz Melissa Bryan Carson, and a bunch of children. Last time I counted Mizz Melissa had given birth to 6 of 'em. Mister John was pretty distraught for a while when I told him Mister James had passed, but he recovered his bearing pretty quickly, and then sent off a telegraph to Mister Carson, which would be received in Reynolds, and then somebody would take it out to the farm.

Mister Carson was sitting on his porch Wednesday afternoon, smoking his pipe in peace in his favorite rocking chair. Enjoying the warm Georgia sun on his face as it was about to set beyond the Pines behind his fields. It had been another hot, sultry day in middle Georgia, and while he was down here, 3 of his boys were up in Virginia, fighting for the Army of Northern Virginia against the hated Yankees. Why couldn't they just leave us alone he thought? "They've already taken my wife from me over worry about this blasted war, and now 3 of my dear sons are smack in the middle of it!" "Lord have mercy!" When Mister Carson looked up, here came old Sam from the telegraph office taking his steed faster than it was ever meant to run, and running right up to his front porch. "Mister Carson, I got a telegram for you suh, thought I'd bring it over myself. I'll wait for your reply if you like suh?" "Huh, oh yes of course, Sam. Please let me read it, and then I'll write up a reply for you."

"My Dear Pop, it is with great sadness that I regret to inform you James has passed away this 27th day of August, in the year of our Lord 1862. He died of Bilious fever after being wounded in battles unknown at the present, though sometime during this summer's campaign.

125

Racked with nausea, vomiting, and diarrhea,
he passed with fidelity, and dignity. He was
proud to contribute to our noble cause. Please
advise on your intentions for his body/burial.

Your mournful son,
John T. Carson CPT CSA

Mister Carson's face turned grey after he read the telegraph, and then he read it a second time then stood up, regained his bearing, and said, "Excuse me a moment Sam while I go write a response to this. I shall return in a minute." "Yes suh, I'll be right heah. Mister Carson went into his library, dipped his favorite pen in ink, and wrote his reply;

Dear J. T., Buy a horse and wagon, and have
George bring James' body back to me post-
haste. Mournfully, J. J. Carson

Mister John showed me his father's reply and said he'd get me a horse and wagon, straw and oats for the horse, and enough victuals for the way back to Reynolds. He also would hand me a wad of money big enough to take me all over the country. That night Mister John found me at the hospital, and had a sturdy enough wagon to handle the trip back to Georgia no problem, along with it he had a Black horse pulling it. The biggest horse I had ever seen, and beautiful! Lawd, what a horse! "George, the body is in the back of the wagon, wrapped up and all, so if you get back within a week, that'd be fine.

The wagons also loaded up with straw and oats for the horse. It belonged to Captain McMillan, so he won't be needing it anymore. There is also enough victuals to get you back to Pop and Lula for a week, so you should be okay on food. Here, take this money." With that he handed a wad of money that was so big, he had to use both of his massive hands! "That should be more than enough to get you home.

Keep what you don't spend you don't have to pay it back." Later when I checked it, it was $1,000 confederate dollars. Lawd have mercy, I'd never in my life held that much money in my own hands before. "George, as soon as you get James back, and get caught up with Lula can you come back?

Say in about a month?" That should be more than enough time to get there and back and catch up with everybody back at home, so I said, "Yes suh. Absolutely,

I'll get back as soon as I can with Captain McMillan's horse and wagon." "Thank you George, thank you so much, "With that he shook my hand, and before he could burst into tears, he jogged off back to his men in the camp.

It was getting dark outside the hospital, so I just bedded down there for the night, right outside the hospital, planning on leaving at first light. After looking at my pocket watch, I noticed it was already 8:30 at night, so after a good night's sleep, the horse and I, and Mister James' body should be on the road by 5 am when the sun starts to peak around the edge of the countryside, when it's nice and cool, and the dew is still on the ground.

As I got out my bedroll and looked at the stars, it seemed like thousands up there in the great big sky, maybe millions of 'em. Who could tell? After I said my prayers, I closed my eyes and went to sleep. As old as I am, that ain't no hard task. After a long day's work, a man my age can close his eyes at night, and then the next thing he knows it's already morning again.

At 4:30 in the morning I couldn't sleep anymore, so I got up and said my prayers, and fed the horse. After about 45 minutes, the sun was beginning to peak up in the eastern sky, and we were on our way back home to Georgia. This war's gone and brought more and more sadness upon Mister Carson and his family. Hopefully nobody else will have to die to satisfy the Yankee hordes. The sun rose quick, and it was good that I had my straw hat on, for if not that hot Ole Virginny sun would a beat down upon my old head something fierce.

It'll be good to get home and see Lula and Mister Carson. Hopefully he's not too maudlin, but who could blame him if he is. Lawd have mercy, he just lost his beloved wife after many years and his second son. "Dear Lawd, please give me success on my journey back to Reynolds Father, keep me safe, and help me to get there fast oh Lawd. In Jesus' great name I beseech thee Father, Amen."

That horse Mister John got me was something else, black as the ace of spades, and strong as an ox. After we stopped to rest a few times, I asked him if he wanted to rest some more, and he said no suh, he was anxious to get back to Reynolds as well. After lunch we passed Danville, VA, and some soldiers from North Carolina marching in a column of twos up to northern Virginia. They didn't molest me at all, and when they found out I was transporting one of their fallen Confederates they bade me safe travel, and asked me if I needed any provisions, and I thankfully said I had everything I needed. After we crossed into North Carolina, things seemed to be quieter than they had been in hectic Virginia. Folks were a little more easy going. Around 5:00 o'clock in the afternoon, the horse and I made it to Greensboro, N.C., and decided to set up camp for the night on the outskirts of town. Mister John had given me letters in case anyone stopped me on the coastal highway.

After feeding the horse, and giving it plenty of water, he was ready to lay down and take a rest. What am I gonna call you big fella? Oscar? No. King Jethro? Hmmm, no, not King Jethro. Samson? Maybe, let me think about it. Though I liked the sound of it, I reckoned I'd dwell on it later. After sleeping another peaceful night under the stars, we set out, and by the end of the day had passed Columbia, South Carolina and decided to settle down for the night. Did I really want to name that horse "King Jethro?" After a day I still wasn't sure. Maybe after sleeping over it another night I can decide. When I woke up I decided his name was gonna be Jethro, just plain Jethro. We don't have kings in America, no need for 'em. They can have all the kings they want in England, but not here. Jethro and I set off, and were grateful for another good night's sleep, good weather, and nobody messing with us. We made it to Augusta, Georgia by night fall after our third day of travel, and Jethro was doing fantastic. That horse could run all day, and *all night if he wanted too*! We were back in our home state of Georgia, and we were both glad.

We hadn't been back home in Georgia for over a year now, and were glad to see red Georgia clay, and a stray cotton field here and there. Though whereas before the war cotton was all you saw in the fields wherever you looked, these days farmers were planting vegetables, and wheat instead to feed the South due to the Yankee blockade of the South. Many were afraid that if the South was unable to break the blockade, the South would eventually starve! Lawd have mercy, can you imagine that? All those years when we almost had *too much to eat* and now the Yankees were systematically starving us.

After feeding Jethro and watering him I ate some ramrod rolls, along with some sorghum that I heated up over the fire. After supper I reached in my gunny sack, and pulled out my tobacco pouch. After loading my pipe, and lighting it, I leaned back against a pine tree and scratched my back. It was good to be back home, but now that we were actually in Georgia, I was most anxious to get home to Lula and Mister Carson. The next 36 hours were a blur after sleeping, and then traveling a long way again the next day, and then the final night's sleep before we made it to Reynolds.

We spend the final night on the road in Sparta, Georgia. Kind of like Reynolds, not much too it, but the folks were nice. Especially after they learned I was taking Mister James back home. They asked me if I needed anything, and I told them thank you, but the good Lawd has taken good care of me. "Well don't be afraid to ask for any help if you need any George." "Yes ma'am, thank you very kindly."

After a peaceful night's sleep, Jethro and I were gonna be home by nightfall, and we were both excited about that. "Dear Lawd, thank you very kindly for helping us to make it thus far. Please get us back home safe and sound. We thank thee for all thy many blessings. In Jesus' great name we ask thee Lawd, Amen."

Chapter 7

It was Monday morning now, September 1, 1862 as we passed through Milledgeville, and then Macon, and they didn't look too much changed from the war. I reckon that's 'cause there hadn't been any fighting through here yet. As Jethro and I continued south, I wondered whether the war would ever make it this far south, and if they did whether we could hang on against the Yankees. Though we sure were determined to win, the Yankees seemed to have way more men and supplies than the South, and if we can't defeat that blockade, that might be the end of the war for us logistically.

"Well lookee heah, Jethro! The Flint River! If that ain't a sight for sore eyes, I don't know what is." After crossing the ferry, I can't tell you how great it felt to be on the Fall Line Highway. Although, I couldn't say the same for the gnats, they still felt too familiar to me, like they were a part of me or I of them. Just like we were both part of this beloved red Georgia clay. It was about 6:30 when we made it to River Road. It was then that I experienced a small amount of sadness, for though the once great plantations didn't appear to be in disarray, they were noticeably less well maintained than they normally were. Maybe with all the men off fighting the Yankees, their wives were unable to do as good of a job as their husbands were. This made me wish the war was over as well, so everybody could come back home and tend to their houses and their land.

But, then I realized I was home. There was Carson House, and mine out back! Mister Carson on the porch in his usual spot smoking his pipe, yelled, "George! Well done my friend. Glad you're back!" Lula was on the porch sweeping, but when she heard him say this, she said, *"GEORGE, IS DAT REALLY YOU HONEY?"* And with that she sprinted over to our wagon, and jumped up on me before I even had a chance to stop and gave me the biggest hug and kiss she'd ever given me. It felt great to be in the arms of the woman you love on the land you love. "It's great to see you Baby! So good to see you again, feels like it's been a hundred years!" "I know Baby, I know. Are you hungry?" "Yes ma'am, I could go for a little supper if you got anything to eat." "Hold on, George, I'll go fix you something right up."

As Lula ran back inside the house, Mister Carson walked up to me and gave me a bear hug, and I hugged him back. For a second I thought he might weep, but he didn't. When he let me go he said, "Thank you very kindly, George, for bringing James back from this awful war! Lord knows if the South doesn't have a quick victory, the Yankees I'm afraid will crush us! Take James and the wagon out back to the barn. I'm going over to Reverend Glover's house and tell him James' funeral will be tomorrow at 11 o'clock. Please get Sam and Henry over to the cemetery and have 'em dig a grave for James' casket." "Yes suh, we'll take care of it for you." "Thank you, George."

After I dropped the wagon off in the barn and fed Jethro, I let Jethro wander around the pasture. Then Sam, Henry, and I went over to the cemetery in front of the house, and all three of us dug a grave big enough for Mister James' casket to go into. Now being thoroughly tired, I went home and was almost too tired to eat. That is until I saw the plate Lula had fixed for me, dripping with gravy. Lawd have mercy! "It was worth the wait,

Honey, to eat your blessed supper!" "Wait to you see what fo dessert, Honey."

It was good to be home, even if it weren't for long. The next morning everyone put on their Sunday finest, and after a while it was time for the funeral. Poor Mister Carson, having to go to two funerals in a three month span for his beloved wife, and then for his not even turned 30 yet son James. He was seated, along with James' widow Melissa, both of them dressed in black. James' children were also seated. It just occurred to me that Mizz Melissa's only 24 years young, and now she's a grieving widow. Lawd have mercy! The rest of us were standing, and I was glad it wasn't so hot today, 'cause if it were some of them fine ladies dressed to the hilt in their Pannier Fashion might faint. After a brief eulogy filled with compassion and grace, Reverend Glover said, "*Let us pray. Almighty God, maker of heaven and earth. You're the wise, all knowing God of heaven, and of earth. We thank thee for thy memory of thy servant James Alston Carson. Lord we thank thee that we know thy servant is in Providence with thee Father and we thank thee for his legacy. We thank thee for the contribution thy servant made for thy kingdom. Now Lord, we beseech thy great name that thou would make this ungodly conflagration come to an abrupt halt. Humbly we beseech thee to end this war soon, Father, for we fear many more of these funerals for thy servants, should it not come to an end soon. Humbly we ask thee to give thy peace to Mrs. Melissa, and comfort her in her loss. In thy name of Jesus we ask all these things, Lord Amen.*"

After the funeral, we went back to the Carson House. Mizz Melissa came up to me and said, "Thank you so much George for bringing James' body back from Virginia." She had to wipe her nose and eyes with her handkerchief, then continued, "He really loved you, George! Talking about all the times y'all went hunting, and fishing when he was growing up." "Well thank you Mizz Melissa.

Mister James was a fine man, and it's such a shame he departed this earth at such a young age." "I know it, George, and now I have all these rascals to take care of, and I don't know what I'm gonna do." She started to cry, so I said, "There, there Mizz Melissa, it's gonna be all right. Don't cry. When the war's over I'll take your boys hunting and fishing, the same as I did for their father when he was their age." "Would you? That would be grand, George! Thank you so much, George." "It's my pleasure, ma'am."

My time home came and went. By the time I was getting used again to Lula's cooking, it was time to go back. Lula started to cry when I got up on Jethro and started to go. "Don't cry baby, I'll be back soon, and then everything will all be back to normal. In the meantime, you take care of Mister Carson. He needs you. I love you." Lula wiped her eyes off with her sleeve, blew her nose into her handkerchief, then said, "I will, Honey. You be good, and come back quick ya heah?" "Yes ma'am, I will!" "I love you, George!"

Last night, Mister Carson and I had a long, good conversation. He was worried about John Thomas and Joseph being harmed next. "They're all I got left, George, besides Robert, and if this blasted war lasts another two years, then Robert will enlist, and then I'll be all alone. George, you take good care of John Thomas, you hear?" "Yes suh, I will." "I know you will. George, I've really enjoyed talking with you about the war and Virginia and all that the last two weeks, but, before I say goodnight, promise me one thing." "Yes suh, anything." "George, promise me that should death take my son John Thomas, like it took my son James that you'll bring him back to me, same as you did for James. You don't have to send a telegraph to ask, just bring him home to

Georgia." "Yes suh, you have my word." "Thank you my friend," he said as we shook hands, "May God grant you protection on your way back to John Thomas, and may y'all come home soon, and in one piece." "Thank you, suh, goodnight."

Chapter 8

J ethro was well rested after two weeks of being back home and ready to use all that energy he had. He was glad to not have to pull the wagon, and so was I. Sitting in that wagon seat for 5 days straight was starting to give me lumbago. I reckon a saddle might be a little more comfortable. John Thomas sent me a telegram last week, and said they were headed towards Greenbrier River, Camp Bartow, that's on the western side of Virginia. Mister Carson telegrammed him back and said that I would be along shortly. On my second day headed towards Virginia, I stopped at nighttime outside of a town called Lavonia, GA. As I was riding by the house of a man who lived on a steep hill, up there where the North Georgia Mountains start, out came a big man, with a stomach bigger than I've ever seen, with a beard to match. "What do you want, boy?" "Hello suh, my horse needs some straw, and water. I just need a place to spend the night. The barn would be fine. I got plenty of money, suh." "We don't get many runaway slaves up in these parts boy. Had one come through here last year, but his master caught him. Took him back. Yes suh, he got him. Now if you ain't no runaway, how comes you're master ain't with you then?" "Suh, that's 'cause I'm going to *him*. He's up in Virginia, fighting the Yankees, and his younger brother James just died, and I brought him home to be buried."

"You brought him back all the way from Ole Virginny, when all you had to do was ditch his body, and go into Pennsylvania so you could be free? That don't make no sense atall." "Suh, it ain't like that with Mister Carson. He gave me my own house, and a little plot of land for a garden. I learned how to read and write, and before the war, we was never hungry, *ever*. My wife and kids are back in Reynolds, as well as my grandchildren. I'm about to be a greatgrandfather suh. So the thought of ditching Mister James' body was the furtherest thing from my mind. Reynolds is my home." "Huh. You say you got money?" "Yes suh, I got plenty of it. Just need some food, and water for my horse and a place to stay for me, and something to eat if that's all right." "Yeah,

I reckon I don't see why you can't stay for the night. I might just be crazy enough to believe you after all." He walked up to me in his overalls. It looked like that was all he had on. No shirt, no shoes, & no socks. He had a long beard and long hair that was starting to go grey. He walked down the hill with a slight limp that he managed with a big stick. "The name's 'Crazy Charlie,'" except he pronounced Charlie, "*Cholly.*" He stuck out his hand while I said, "Yes suh, I'm George Carson, sho nuff a pleasure to meet you." "Likewise George, and calling me suh is like calling an outhouse, Windsor Castle. The two just don't go together. Charley, or Crazy Charley will do just fine." "Pleased to meet you, Charley."

"George, if you wanna get that beautiful animal of yours fed and settled for the night, I'll go stir us up something to eat." "Thank you, Charley, I'll be right up, soon as Jethro is looked after." "Good. When you come up you don't have to knock, just come on in." "Yes s... Charley." "There you go again, George. But, I won't hold it against you." I smiled at him, and went back to the barn. At first Mister Charley seemed kind of scary, but I'll bet that side of him was just for strangers, and folks he didn't care for. Otherwise, I got the feeling he was a fun gentleman to be around.

After Jethro was fed and bedded down for the night I went up to the house, and walked right in. "Have a seat George, I was just about to eat supper when you rode up." "Thanks Charley." And I went to the place he'd set for me. Charley said a quick grace, and then we started eating. "This is delicious. Can I give the recipe to my wife?" "Sure there, George, this right heah is barbecued venison, and the stew is also venison brunswick stew." This sure was good. I'll have to get Lula to make some. I dipped my corn bread in the stew, and took a bite. "My wife died about 5 years ago this October I believe. She just up and died one morning. Doctor didn't know why, or how. Just said he didn't know why, that's all." "I'm sorry to hear that, Charley. That happened to Mister Carson's wife 3 months ago. Then with his son dying and all, and the others ones off fighting, it ain't good. No suh, ugh, sorry, I mean Charley." Charley laughed. "It's quite all right George. I thought about getting another one, but I reckon I'll wait 'til I find one that can cook as good as Ludmilla did." He patted his ample belly, and said, "Before we got married 30 years ago I weighed 147 lbs. Can you believe it?" No, I certainly couldn't believe it, but I took his word for it. "By the time she passed, my pant size had doubled in the waist!" But I didn't complain since I was never at want for something good to eat, 3 times a day, 7 days a week, 52 weeks in a year. Good Lawd, could that woman cook!"

"I'm sure your wife was an excellent cook Charlie, no doubt about it. But, if you ever come through Reynolds, you oughtta come by my house and try my wife Lula's cooking. Why half of South Georgia has visited her kitchen this year alone!" "My word, George, she must be if all 'em folks keep visiting her kitchen. But how come you don't seem to retain most of it like I do?" "That's a good question Charley. Often wondered the same myself. Reckon it's 'cause most of my life, 6 days of the week I'm out hunting, or fishing, horseback riding, or something. You reckon that's how I kept it off?" "Mmm hmmm.

Must be, 'cause I don't leave the house that often myself, most of the time I stay in heah in my cabin and read. Got me a little garden out back of the cabin where I grow all my vegetables."

We finished up our wonderful supper, cleaned the table, and then retired to a couple of chairs by the fire. Charlie smoking his corn cob pipe, and me smoking my briar pipe. "That tobacco smells good. Where'd you get it?" "This is called Virginia Cavendish, Charley, & they make it up there in Ole Virginny." I took out my tobacco pouch and offered it to Charley, "Here, have some. It tastes good too." Charley emptied his pipe out into the fire, put Virginia Cavendish in his, and lit it up. "Hey, you warn't teasing nuther! That's the best pipe tobacco I ever had. Thank you George!" "My pleasure s...I mean Charley." He laughed at that. "I understand all them planters down in middle and south Georgia, why they're all genteel, and refined like. Up here where the mountains start to form, they call us folks Hill Billy's. Reckon we're about as different as apples and oranges." I thought about that, "at least we're both from the great state of Georgia." "You're right about that, George." I got something stuck in my throat, and coughed. I coughed a few more times 'til I noticed that jar of water he had on the mantle of his fireplace. "Excuse me Charley," I croaked hoarsely, "could I please have some of your water in that jar please?" With that request Charley laughed out loud. "Sure you can have some George. It's got water in it, but it ain't exactly the kind you get out the river." My throat felt so sore I thought I was gone die! I needed some of that water or whatever it was right now. Hoarsely I said, "That's all right. May I please have some?" Charley went and grabbed it from the mantle, but he said, "Don't drink it too fast though." I opened the jar, and it smelled like water to me, so I took as big of a gulp as I dared. Half of it went down my throat, and immediately my stomach felt like it was on fire. So the other half I spit into the fire without thinking. It felt like my body was being controlled by someone else, for I'd never spit on anyone's floor like that.

When I spit the "water" into the fire, the fire tripled in size for a few seconds, and then pretty quickly returned back to its normal height. Charley laughed, and laughed. "Shoulda told you what it was first, George." While my head slowly stopped spinning round in huge circles, I asked him, "What in the world was that?" "They call it shine. Some folks call it "moon shine," though I never found out why." He smiled, "Did you like it?" My belly was still on fire, and my head was still spinning. "Umm, can't say that I did, Charley." He chuckled, "Would you like some real water, George, or some tea?" "No thank you, Charley."

Chapter 9

The next morning I got up early and packed up the horse, and said good bye to Charley. I tried to thank him by paying him for the food and lodging, but he wouldn't hear of it. "What kind of a Christian would I be if I charged a stranger for food and shelter when he didn't have any? Good luck, George, stop by on your way back if you come through these here parts." I shook his hand then said, "Much obliged, Charley. God bless you."

The rest of the trip went as smoothly as the first part. I didn't know if Charley was playing a joke on me or what with that shine. Boy, that stuff might be poison or something. Reckon it'll likely kill children and old folks.

I made it to Camp Bartow on Wednesday, September 24, 1862. When I found Mister John he was glad to see me. He asked me how everyone was back home was, and how Mister Carson, and Mizz Melissa were getting along.

"They're doing as good as could be expected of 'em," I said. "We've been here a few weeks now, George, and the men seem to enjoy this place. We expect the Yankees to attack pretty soon, just not sure when though."

The Battle of Greenbrier River could be called a draw since both sides had about the same number of men killed in action and wounded in action. Except I ain't real sure how you can call it a draw when the Yankees had nearly 3 times more men than the South had on the battlefield. Luckily Mister John wasn't wounded. Although sanitary conditions at our camp at Greenbrier River were so unsanitary, that 8 of our soldiers died of disease in camp. The men called it "Camp Death" because of the wretched conditions. And these men weren't dying of bullet wounds necessarily, but they were dying of wretched diseases. Gangrene and all kinds of horrible diseases killed these fine young men.

After this horrible battle, autumn was a coming and with it cooler weather. At first those nights were sweet, after the roaring heat of the Virginia countryside in the summer. But after the middle of October, those hills were freezing at night. Had to sleep by the fire to stay warm, otherwise you felt like you were gonna freeze to

death. To make matters worse, that was *fall weather.*
Winter hadn't even come yet, and it was a coming.

The young men didn't mind the colder weather, didn't
bother 'em a bit. But, it bothered my joints. Especially
before sunrise, Mister John said he could hear my joints
pop clear across camp, and he was so sorry I had to
endure the misery of camp life, but he was grateful for
my company though.

We often talked about Joe and Robert, and wondered
what they were up to. Joe was off somewhere with 4th
Georgia Regiment, Company I. Mister Carson said he
commanded the Sharpshooters. An elite unit of men
who could shoot their Whitworth rifles through a silver
dollar from 1,800 yards! I thought I was a pretty good
shot, and I was the one who taught Joseph how to shoot!
Lawd have mercy! Rifles that can shoot that far out
ought to shoot their way up the east coast, all the way
to the White House.

Winter came and passed in 1863, and thank
goodness! We liked to freeze to death. But, all the men
knew that spring meant time to go back to fighting.
The new boy recruits fresh from home, with their shiny
butternut colored uniforms said they were "ready for
war! I'm gonna kill me a Yank, George, if it's the last

thing I ever do!" The veterans were a lot more leery, for their hearts were still in it, but combat had made 'em much more conservative in their approach than their green counterparts.

These rookie soldiers got their chance to finally fight the hated Yankees at Chancellorsville, VA., towards the middle of May in 1863 as I recall. General Lee split his forces in the face of the Army of the Potomac which was more than double his own, and therefore able to achieve an impressive victory. On the heels of this impressive victory, Mister John was promoted to Major on Tuesday June 9th, 1863.

I missed home, and so did Mister John. As our Army marched through Northern Virginia, we landed in the Pennsylvania town of Gettysburg and fought one of our most even handed fights with the Yankees we had fought so far. The Army of the Potomac had 90,000 men, while the Army of Northern Virginia had 75,000 young troopers. After General Lee's failed attempts to flank the Yankees, we retreated back across the Potomac able to escape from the Federals.

I got a letter from Lula after we got back across the Potomac, written by Mister Carson's newest wife Mizz Mary Laura Lamar Slappey Carson, whom he married not long after his first wife Mizz Martha died. They were married on Tuesday October 21, 1862.

Dear George,

Haven't heard from you in quite a while, I hope all is well. It's been hotter than Hades here this summer. I pray for you every night. Treat Mister John well, and y'all come back soon. Mister Carson is getting along all right after all the sadness this war has brought him.

Love,
Lula

Dear Lula,

We're fine up here in Northern Virginia Honey. Thanks for your prayers, I can feel them working. We'll be home as soon as we can.

Your loving husband of many years,
George

The war didn't seem to be going the way everybody thought it would go at first. Everyone knew the Yankees would be tough, but didn't know they would be this tough. On top of this, nobody counted on a blockade that was crippling the South at a time when it most needed to be broken through.

The men's morale was still high, though they were anxious for a victory that could rally 'em and give 'em some momentum against the Federals. But, without more men they were always undermanned against the Yankees in every battle. Union General Grant said after the war that each rebel soldier was worth three Federal soldiers.

Thus, the Yankees were often reluctant to do prisoner swops with the South, for fear of prolonging the war even more with fresh southern troopers out of prison.

Chapter 10

At the end of November 1863, in the Mine Run campaign, General Meade and the Army of the Potomac were unsuccessful in its attempt to defeat the Army of Northern Virginia, and thus, it marked the end of hostilities between the belligerents for the year. Thus came another Christmas away from home for the men and myself. By now men were starting to get really home sick and tired of being away from home because of the war. They didn't understand why they could never seem to get any traction in defeating the Yankees. Seemed liked every time they took two steps forward, they took three steps backward. The winter of 1864 was nice and quiet, with neither side in the war wanting to fight in the cold. Fighting in the hot, humid summer was bad enough, but, at least you could drink from your canteen, or sit under a tree. I reckon only a Yankee from Minnesota would want to fight in 5 feet of snow, but no Southern man with a brain would be willing to fight in those wretched conditions. Mister John told me the other day when it was 20 degrees, snowing, and real windy, that he heard a Yankee prisoner say, "This weather ain't nothing, Johnny!

Back home in Ohio this weather would be considered a "mild" day." Mister John told him, "Well suh, that doesn't sound like a place that's much fun to be in the winter time then."

Winter came and went, and with it, blessed warmer weather, and the colors of spring made everyone almost forget they were still at war. Back home, Mister Carson was not looking forward to spring, for he knew what was coming with it, and it was with deep sadness and not joy when Saturday April 2nd, 1864 hit that Robert "Bob" Hall Carson enlisted in the 12th Georgia Regiment, Company C. When he came home that night all spiffy in his Butternut C.S.A. Army uniform, Lula said, "Why, Mister Bob, doan you look spiffy in 'dat new uniform you got on!" She came over and gave him a big hug. "Land sakes alive, chile, seem like last week you was knee high to a duck, and now you all growed up. You be careful up dere ya heah?" "I will Lula, thank you for those nice things you said to me. Where's Pop?" "He in his library taking a nap." "Thanks, Lula." "Good evening suh," Bob proclaimed with the best military inflection he could muster. "Well now, Robert don't you look dashing in your new uniform. Your mother, God rest her soul, would be so proud of you." "Thank you suh, it's unfortunate that I can't show it to her. I miss her a lot." "I know you do, son. You were the baby, and you got away with stuff John Thomas, James, and Joseph would've never dreamed of. So, what are the Army's plans for you?" Inwardly Mister Carson hoped they would keep Robert here in Macon County as part of the home guard, but his gut however told him different. "Suh, they gave me orders to report back to 'em no later than 0700 hours Tuesday, to give me enough time to catch the train to Virginia." Good Lord Mister Carson inwardly sighed that they've now taken all my sons from me. "Dear God, please let at least one of my boys come home to me alive from this horrible war, or you can take me whenever you want Lord, 'cause if none of my sons come home alive from this monstrosity of a war, then I'll be ready to go home to you oh Lord."

"Son, sit down." "Yes suh." "Robert, this war has already taken my son James from me, and if you, or

John Thomas, or Joseph should be taken from me as well it would break my old heart. You're young and invincible, and bulletproof in your mind, but you're not, son." "Pop, I don't believe I'm bulletproof...." "Yes, you do son, all young men do, and don't interrupt me until I'm finished. When you get up there to Virginia, I want you to be careful. I have a feeling this awful war will be over in about a year, and the South must be made to pay for it. Most of my peers already know this. It's just that they're not willing to say it out loud, for fear of being unpatriotic. But the fact is this, from all the reports we've been getting for the last 3 years, General Lee has fought a valiant campaign, often times against armies that are twice as large as his. The South has pretty much conceded the fighting out west, yes they're still fighting valiantly, but the writing's on the wall my son. You must at least try to stay alive, my young son, or my heart'll be broken if you return home as your older brother James did in a Pine Box. Now, you're assigned to John Thomas' outfit, the 12th Georgia Infantry Regiment. So you go report tohim in Virginia, but he's going to have you reassigned to Joseph's 4th Georgia Infantry Regiment, Company I, where upon you will be a courier for Generals Dole and Cook,"

"But I don't want to be a courier. Couldn't I at least be a Sharpshooter like Joe?" *"NO SUH! OVER MY DEAD BODY WILL YOU GET YOURSELF THAT CLOSE TO THE ACTION! YOU WILL BE A COURIER FOR GENERALS DOLE & COOK!* Do you understand me, son?" "Yes suh." "Now I know, son, that you're very disappointed, but that is how it's going to be. Son, do you know how many thousands of men have been killed so far?" "No suh, I don't reckon I do." "It is incredible my boy, some say that between 400,000 - 500,000 men of our nation have been killed so far, or will have been killed by the time this terrible war is over. Our nation lost less than 5,000 men in the Revolutionary War, and that was about 3 times longer than we've been fighting this War Between the States, and 100 times the number dead, *so far.*

When you arrive in Virginia, you will inform John Thomas and Joseph when you see them that their direct orders from me are to execute their assigned duties with fidelity and honor, but under no circumstances are y'all to take unnecessary risks that will cause your own death or serious injury. They have already served their nation and their family with honor, and now is the time to start to think about surviving. Now I want you to know that

I'm very proud of you Robert and your Mother would've been too. Go get washed up for supper." "Yes suh, Pop, is it all right if I ask you a question?" "Yes suh, indeed it is. What is it?" "Pop is it okay to be afraid when the Yankees are trying to kill you?" "Robert, I guarantee you that every man up there fighting gets scared every now and then. It's what you do after that that matters. When a man gets afraid, and he succumbs to that fear, then that fear will paralyze him, and he has been effectively taken out of the fight. While the man who while maybe afraid decides to conquer that fear by continuing to fight, he will be victorious over his scared counterpart." "Thanks, Pop." "My pleasure young man, now go get ready for supper. This will be the finest meal you'll have for a long time I'm sure."

After the finest meal Robert had ever remembered, Robert went out onto the front porch with his father and stared at the stars as they appeared. He wondered why he couldn't fight, but realized his Pop was right. He reckoned the war was probably about over, and he didn't want to be one of the 500,000 in a Pine Box. Although he did want to kill a Yank something fierce for what they did by starting the war in the first place and for what they did to James.

Couldn't his Pop understand that? Couldn't he feel the righteous indignation he felt over the Yankees trying to handle all the South's affairs, instead of butting out and minding their own business? He probably did, but he had also contributed so much to the cause himself.

He was about to send his fourth son to the war, and there was no telling if any of the three left would come back. I wonder why Pop never joined the Army? The Revolution was over a long time before he was born. During the war of 1812 he was a lot younger than I am now. Other than the Mexican-American War and now there weren't any other wars he could have fought in. Robert felt lucky to have the honor to serve his nation in the Army, but he wondered if his father *was the lucky one?*

After a breakfast on Tuesday that was better than Lula's "normal" breakfasts, Robert was glad he was leaving, for if he stayed he'd never be able to fit into his uniform again. Riding the train to Virginia with Robert was a Private named James Elliot. Once Robert was able to get away from his Father, he was able to again show the same bravado he'd been showing for the last 3 years.

Chapter 11

During the two day trip he found Private Elliot to be of the same mind, and the two shared a cabin on the train, and quickly become close friends. "How many Yanks you gonna kill in yer first crack at 'em there, Bob?" "Probably won't be able to kill any 'cause my Pop done gone and made me a courier for the Generals! Can you imagine that sorry state of affairs here? I've been waiting 3 years for my turn to go up there to 'Ole Virginny, to show them Yanks a thing or two, and then before I even leave the Great State of Georgia, my Pop pulls a fast one on me, and makes it so I can't be near enough to the front to kill a Federal! However, my brother Joe, he's a Captain over the Sharpshooters, maybe one day I can go out with him on a raid and kill me some Yanks that way. That way my Pop might not even find out 'cause I'd just tell him if he did find out that, "Captain Carson ordered me to do it suh.

Just following orders suh, that's all." James Elliot who said he was the same age as Robert, 18, said he also woke up yesterday morning as an 18 year old man finally, and it's off to war he went. He'd been waiting patiently for three years, same as Bob for his chance at the Yanks, and now he was about to get it.

Both boys had never been outside of Macon County before, so the train ride up to Virginia was a special treat! "Yes suh, I'ma gonna kill me all the Yanks I can in my first battle if I do say so myself! They say the Yankees might be winning the war, but, not after I get ahold of 'em. My Great Grand Pappy, Uriah Oglethorpe Elliot was a Colonel in the Georgia Militia in the Revolutionary War, and my Pappy told me he killed a heep of Redcoats. In fact, he said in one battle with 'em in South Carolina, Camden I reckon he called it, he said his Grandpappy killed so many redcoats that when they was on the ground, and you was looking at 'em from afar, there was so much blood that all a body saw was red. Along with them Redcoats. Yes suh, I reckon that's what happened, and that's what I'ma gonna do to them Yanks. Too much is at stake, Bob. The honor of the South, the State of Georgia, and the Elliot family will be upheld, and we will drive them wretched Yanks back up North to their factories, and their big old cities with carts and buggies, and manure all over the place. No suh, them Yanks can have all that horse manure. You and me Bob, we belong in Macon County, where the Almighty has blessed our people, and if we have to fight to preserve that blessing, then fight we shall."

Bob and James arrived in camp on Thursday April 7, 1864. James soon became known as "Private Big Mouth." Everybody in the 12th appreciated his zeal and his spunk. But truth be known, the young man was really not a young man. In fact he was a young boy. He lied to the recruiters of the 12th Georgia Regiment and told them he had just turned 18.

However, though he was a very large boy at 6 feet 3 inches tall and weighed well over 200 pounds, the lad was in fact barely *16*. Coming from a good Christian family who wouldn't have allowed him to enlist in the C.S.A. Army until 18, he simply woke up one morning, and decided he was going to run away, and go fight the Yankees. The veterans of combat for going on 3 years now told him to shush when he got going too much, and that was usually the end of it.

Mister John was glad to see young Robert, as I was as well. "Robert, what in tarnation happened to you boy? You've doubled since I saw you last!" "It's great to see you too, John, but I go by Bob now, even though Pop don't care much for it." "*Well exccccccccccuse me, Bob.* You look like you've gained 30 pounds since I saw you last. What's Lula been feeding you, Boy?" "It's not what she's been feeding me. It's what Doc Johnson called my second growth spurt. He reckoned some boys don't mature until they're around 15. Then when I turned 16 I finally grew taller than Pop. Boy that was a great day indeed! Although I reckon Lula's cooking did help a little since nobody else is around these days on account of the war. Land sakes alive, the county feels abandoned with everybody up here fighting and all. The women practically let the farms go to rot, for all the inexperience they have in running a plantation, we're lucky we even have any food at all." "How's Pop getting on? Is he still depressed after Mother's passing and James'?" "Naw, I reckon he got over her passing pretty quick, though not near as long as James' though. Some days back then he'd just go out back in the fields and walk all day with that new dog of his and his pipe. Several times I tried to come along to cheer him up, but he wouldn't have none of it. He told me to run along and find something to do. Friends and family came calling on him from Atlanta, Macon, and Savannah to cheer him up. He was pleasant enough I reckon, but I could tell he was mighty uncomfortable, and so could they.

Finally, the word got out, and folks believed it would be best to just let him suffer in silence since nobody made any progress in cheering him up. Then one day when he first met that wife of his it was like he came out of a trance, and next month on October 21st, '62. I remember it because the day they got married same day it rained nearly 6 inches. It was so bad that the road in front of the house was flooded for a week, and I couldn't go to school. That I didn't mind though." "Well, *Bob*, it's so good to see you. Hopefully this everlasting war will be over soon so we can go home. In the meantime, I've got orders for you to carry with you to 4th Georgia Infantry Regiment, Company I, Joseph's outfit. There you'll be a courier for Generals Dole and Cook. Pop warned me in a telegram you were coming up here in a bloodlust, and so I'm here to tell you, *Bob*, that war is awful, boy! The worst! Sometimes when we're asleep at night you'll wake up 'cause half the men are screaming in their sleep at the top of their lungs, "*NNNNNNNNNOOOOOOOOOOOOOOOOO!*" While they dream of watching the Doc cut off their arms or their legs. Or for some of our men, BOTH. We have to get the men so lickered up that they black out, then four men have to hold 'em down while Doc saws off their appendages. The worst is when those strong farm hands who black out wake up not knowing what's going on, and seeing Doc sawing their leg off, then it takes even more men to hold 'em down, or Doc won't be able to work on 'em 'til they got 'em held down correctly. Does that sound glorious to you? Does sleeping with one eye open for three years sound like fun to you? Does fighting all day, and then marching all night for weeks at a time seem like fun to you Boy? Well, it ain't, and I'll tell you what. I'm so proud of these men of mine 'cause everyone of 'em's thinking it too all the time, what I just told you boy. *I THINK IT!* But they don't say it out loud for fear of dispiriting the men. Some days all they'll get to eat all day is a rusk biscuit with Sorghum. And they still have to fight all day and march all night.

These are the finest fighting men you ever saw *Bob*, and it's not just C Company, it's the whole Regiment, the entire Corps, and Army of Northern Virginia as a whole. I reckon if we had as many men as the Yankees we'd have whipped 'em 3 years ago. Word is, Bob, that they have more men, more and better guns, but we have better soldiers. Yankees are fighting because they were drafted, or they didn't have a mill or factory job, so they needed the money. Not us, Bob, for we're fighting for a cause we believe in enough to leave our farms and families and be gone for years on end if necessary. That cause of ours gives us a big advantage over the Federals, I reckon. A man won't fight and die for Shinplasters, but he will for a *cause*

It's good to see you, Boy, or I should say man 'cause you're all growed up. Looky here, I've dispatched two Sergeants to take you to your outfit at 0300 hundred hours. Hang around here in this area until then. You can sleep, or eat, whatever you want. Though let me give you some good advice, Bob. Until this war, is over I highly suggest you do both of those things when you can. Sleep when you can, and eat when you can. One day you'll be sitting there on a Sunday morning writing letters home instead of eating, and next thing you know, some Yankee spots us and leads an attack on us, and now you gotta fight all day, and sometimes all night with an empty stomach. Even though you're young and don't need as much sleep as I do, do it anyway. Especially after all the fighting and marching, it wears a body out, and Doc says that sleep will help heal the body. Try to write your letters during the day, 'cause nighttime is for sleeping. Understood?" "Yes, suh." "Good. Good to see you, brother, but I've got to go over a battle plan with my executive officer." With that they shook hands, and Mister John was off to see his X.O., that is what we called him for short.

Chapter 12

On May 5-6th, the Regiment fought splendidly at the Battle of Wilderness, and then continued fighting the Yankees for about two weeks at Spotsylvania Court House. While the South was outnumbered two to one, they fought bravely and valiantly. Although the battle had 32,000 casualties that made it have the fourth highest amount of casualties in a battle in the entire war. Luckily Mister John wasn't wounded in any of those battles. The other day he got a letter from his wife Mizz Susan. You shoulda seen the look on that man's face when I handed him the letter, and he saw it was from his wife. Most men don't have a look like that of puppy love when they've been married as long as they have, 17 years and going strong. 'Course the last 3 of 'em they've been separated.

Saturday June 18, 1864

My Dear Husband John Thomas,

We received your letter dated June 7th and were so thrilled to hear from you! Even though your men seem to be involved in a lot of fighting, we're so proud of y'all for your fidelity to our cause and your rock solid commitment to the South. I miss you so much, but, at the same time I can't tell you how proud I am of you.

Three long years of being separated from your arms has in a strange way made me feel closer to you than ever before. Things have changed here dramatically since you were here last. The dreaded blockade of the South is having a devastating effect on us back on the home front. Food supplies are at an all time low, and what food we do have now is a paltry reminder to the good fortune heaven had always blessed us with before the war. Lord, how we all pray that there will be a quick end to this horrible war, and all the lonely wives may be reunited with their soldier heros!

In closing my love, please pay close attention here. With James already a victim of the war, your father and I are concerned that with young Robert enlisting, our good fortune regarding you and Joseph may change if the fighting doesn't end too soon. My dear John Thomas fight valiantly for us, and for the honor of our cause, but, darling, please, please don't take any chances after the good Lord has kept you safe thus far. Thank you dear one for heeding this call.

I wish with all I have right now that if I had just one last wish, it would be that you would wrap me up in your great big arms like you always do and not let go. Oh, John Thomas my love, I declare, my emotions are getting the best of me now. Stay safe, sugar. All your family is so proud that their Major John Thomas Carson is fighting for them against the Yankees. Give all my love to our dear George. Thank heaven for his kind, and gentle soul.

Your loving wife of 17 wonderful years,
Susan

The 12th Regiment was involved in a lot of skirmishes and battles in the summer of '64. After three days of battle at Cold Harbor on June the first through the third, and trust me, it definitely wasn't *cold, probably 'cause it's real cold there in the wintertime I reckon.* Afterwards it was on to the Lynchburg campaign which took up part of May and June of 1864. July 9th foundthem in Frederick, Maryland fighting at Monocacy, with General Jubal A. Early trying to distract the Federals away from General Lee's Army which was under siege at Petersburg, VA. The raid was a success, and the men were happy to earn a victory, no matter how small it may be.

Chapter 13

After the raid came the quiet before the storm. The men wouldn't see any action again until the Third Winchester campaign on September 19th. Most of the veterans who had been there the whole time took big advantage of this time. It was during this summer lull that Private James "Loudmouth" Elliot went AWOL (absent without leave) on June 27th, 1864, and nobody heard from him again until August 31, *or missed him.* He told his buddy Private Bradberry that he couldn't take it anymore and had to get out of there before he got killed. "John, I can't take it anymore. I gotta get outta here before some lucky Yank sends me on to glory."

It came about that they made it as far as Greensboro, N.C. until they were rounded up by a couple of Sergeants in the North Carolina Home Guard. One of their tasks, aside from guarding against theft and looting, was to be on the lookout for deserters from the Army. They were often easy to spot, for their clothes were filthy, they had no money, food, and little water. In Greensboro when they were asked to produce a copy of their orders they would mumble, "Orders? What's orders?" At that point they had several choices after a quick interrogation it was easily discovered they were deserters. One, they could get a new/used uniform, complete with boots, a good meal, and a train ticket back to their unit. The first option was usually the best option, and 9 out of 10 deserters wisely chose it. The second option if they refused to return to their unit was court martial, with whatever punishment would be meted out. Finally, should a court martial not be available, deserters were incarcerated and often put outside for long hours at a time on chain gangs doing menial tasks beneath even a slave.

Often times especially when out in public, these deserters were subject to the worst kind of verbal and physical abuse which occurs in the lowest Saloons and Taverns at waterfronts throughout the world. For the war had caused sweet Southern ladies with husbands, brothers, and sons off fighting for their way of life to completely forget their devotion to the almighty and his son, and go off on tangents on these poor deserters, using words a gentleman would never dream of using in a lady's hearing. Such was the rancor and vitriolic speech coming from these formerly kind natured, good mannered, genteel women that oftentimes it only took one of these scathing rebukes for these cowards on the chain guards to beg the guards to let them go back and fight. Right then and there! After a while this began to be the general trend, with over 90% of the deserters returning to their units with a change in their hearts on the war, and a fire in their belly.

Only 10% of the most vile, no count, low down, good for nothing, yellow belly cowards accepted this scorn gladly instead of going to help their dying comrades in arms. This fact alone earned these good for nothings heap upon heaps of abuse. They were forced to shovel horse and cow manure 12 hours a day, and the other twelve hours were subjected to more verbal tongue lashings from the sweet old lady Sunday School Teachers, who considered these men worse than vermin.

When the two deserters returned, Major Carson saw no need to charge the men as deserters in a court martial, for after them telling him what they endured in Greensboro, it was all he could do not to laugh out loud in front of them. I was there when they came to him, and I'll never forget Mister John laughing hysterically when they were dismissed! War is a funny thing. Things are funny that wouldn't be funny during times of peace, and vice versa.

Mister John and his troopers had a kind of a lull in the fighting in August, but September would bring much more heavy fighting. The Yankees, led by General Phil Sheridan, attacked General Jubal A. Early and his men at Winchester, VA on Monday September 19th, 1864. The attacking Yankee Army was over three times larger than General Early's. General Gordon's division, which included the 12th Georgia Regiment, was pushed hard into battle from the North, and stuck out on the Confederate left flank, alongside elements of the 22nd Virginia Infantry, who were commanded by Colonel George S. Patton.

It was a beautiful day, and not a cloud in the sky, and the temperature was just right, after a brutally hot summer. As the Yankees kept advancing, the Confederate line held against relentless pressure. During one of the initial advances by the Yankees, Mister John was struck by a Yankee bullet that went right through his leg. Luckily for him it didn't hit a bone or anything. The Regimental Surgeon patched him up, and he was back into the fight.

I reckon that was about 10 a.m. when he was first struck. Being outmanned and outgunned, the Army of Northern Virginia fought valiantly and with great fidelity. However, pretty soon they became overwhelmed after the Yankees superior numbers began to wear out the outnumbered Rebels. About 3 p.m. Mister John was shot again in his arm. The Surgeon wanted to operate on him, but Mister John told him, "No thank you, suh. I must get back in the fight and lead my men. When this battle is over I shall attend to my medical needs, but not while my men are fighting for their lives out there. Good day suh."

Around 6 p.m., General Gordon sounded a retreat, and with that the South tried desperately to regroup, and regather to be able to fight another day. Mister John and his men were in full retreat, hurrying to avoid the cascade of Federal bullets and shells. The Veterans of the war retreated in a disciplined, orderly manner. While the soldiers who had recently been assigned to the Regiment, and Company C were screaming for their lives, *"The Yankees are gonna kill us all. The Yankees are gonna kill us all! Run for your lives!!!"*

It was at this point in the retreat that advancing Federal troops shot Mister John in the stomach, and he went down hard. Unable to walk, two of his men carried him out of the battle, while 10 of his best shooters formed a V around him and protected him so they could concentrate on carrying Mister John out as fast as possible, and the ones who were carrying him not have to worry about firing their rifles as well.

When they safely made it back to the Surgeon he asked him if he could talk. "Barely," replied Mister John. "Sergeant, hand me that Swoon Bottle yonder!" "Yes suh, heah suh." "John Thomas, drink as much of this as you can. Take your time."

Mister John took a big gulp, and nearly spit it all out, but managed to swallow half of it. He took another big sip from the bottle, but this time he didn't spit any out. He continued this until he drank the contents of the entire bottle. Then his eyes glazed over, and he saw me. "George, George" and he reached out his hand towards me. "Am I gonna die, George?" "No suh, the Surgeon's gonna take real good care of you. Now try to relax Mister John. He said they're gonna take you to the hospital at Lynchburg." "Good, good. I feel a little better already." "Well now, that's good to hear, Mister John. They're gonna take real good care of you, and you'll be ready to come back and fight in no time."

There were many wounded on both sides of this battle, including the Commander of the 22nd Virginia Infantry, Colonel George S. Patton who would never wear the star of Brigadier General for which he was recently approved, since he died in the battle

We arrived at the military hospital in Lynchburg, VA at 3:00 on Tuesday afternoon. It was an atmosphere of bedlam in the hospital, *"Doctor, doctor." "What is it nurse, I'm busy?" Doctor, where do I put this triple amputee; there's nowhere for him to lie down." "I don't know. Put him on the floor. I've got to do a surgery. Ask somebody else."*

That's what we were greeted with after the chaotic train ride up here to Northern Virginia. The coach we were on was packed with soldiers standing up and down the aisle with nowhere to sit, and every single one of 'em was wounded in some form or fashion. Mister John tried to stand at first to allow soldiers who were worse off than him a seat, but 45 minutes after we departed he collapsed into my arms, and I was able to find a seat for him in the caboose.

Lack of beds, medicine, and food caused by the war and the blockade of the South had tied the doctors and nurses hands behind their backs.

They really did care for their patients, but with so many of 'em, and a lack of supplies and resources they did yeoman's work in saving as many patients as they could. Mister John was admitted to the hospital and received a room on the second floor in what was formerly the "White Sulfur Resort" before the war.

In his room were 3 other officers, and space was tight. After I got Mister John settled in his bed was when I first noticed the smell of this place. I had smelled it before on the farm when a cow, or a hog, or chicken got sick. It was the smell of DEATH. The other three officers in the room were all asleep and seemed to be at peace. One of 'em had no legs. Another had no legs, and one arm had been cut off. The third one had no arms and no legs. Lawd have mercy!

"George, I'm famished. You reckon you could scrounge up some victuals for me?" Out in the hallway I found a handsome nurse, probably no older than Mister Robert at her desk busily going through her reports, looking frustrated, and flustered.

"Pardon me, ma'am, may I inquire of you where to get some victuals for Major Carson? I reckon he hasn't eaten in quite a while, and he's got three gunshot wounds in him. Reckon he needs to build up his strength." The nurse looked me over real good, and then she smiled at me. "What is your name Mister?" "Ma'am, my name is Mister George Carson. I hail from Reynolds, GA, and I've been looking after Mister Carson and his younger brothers since they were knee high to a duck. If you could help me ma'am I'd greatly appreciate it. If you're unable to I understand, and I can fend for myself." "Well now, that's really sweet of you to look after Major Carson and his brothers since they were little boys. I tell you what, suppertime ain't 'til 5:00, and it's only 3:30. My name is Lead Nurse Miss Ophelia Johnson.

Run down to the mess hall on the first floor, and tell 'em Lead Nurse Miss Ophelia Johnson from amputation wing sent you down, and if they give you any hassles report back to *me pronto.*" "Yes, ma'am, thank you ma'am!" I made it to the mess hall with ease. All a body had to do was be led by his nose, and the nose would take you right to it. When I arrived at the mess hall I was greeted by an arrogant, ornery black man who seemed to feel he was better than everybody else. He seemed to be in charge of the place, so I walked right up to him and polite as I could said, "Hi, I was told this is where I could get some food for Major John Thomas Carson. He just checked in to the hospital and hasn't had anything to eat in a day and a half, and he's injured and all, so I was hoping to get him something in his stomach as soon as I could."

"Well now," he said, "ain't that special. It ain't my problem he ain't ate in that long. He can wait 'til 5 like everybody else." This devil minded young rascal was about to get on my last nerve, and then he said, "This is my mess hall. Nobody gets special run of the place lessen he goes through me. I'm what they call a newly freed black man. Nobody comes in here at 3:45, an hour and 15 minutes before supper demanding special treatment from me 'cause they ain't ate in a long time. They pay me to run this place suh. And they don't pay me in Confederate dollars, which is worthless. They pay me in Shinplasters, greenbacks, dollar bills. My wife and I got me a little place outside of town. She ain't free yet, but she will be soon. Say where you from old man?" By now my *"old blood"* was starting to pump much faster and hotter. Dear Lawd in heaven please let me keep my cool, and not lather this young scamp out back where nobody can see me. Thank you Lawd, Amen. "I hail from the Great State of Georgia suh, and this *old man* would appreciate a little respect from you, *sonny.*" "GEORGIA! Hmph! What's so great about Georgia? I came through there on my way up here with my Master Colonel Wilbur Anderson.

When he got kilt by the Yankees, they caught me and said I was free as a bird, and I could go wherever I wanted. Since this hospital's used by both North and South, they said I could work in the mess hall as a free man if I chose too, so I told 'em, "yes suh, be happy to do it." 'Cept I reckon I didn't have to call him suh anymore since I was free as him now and all. You got an apartment back in the great state of Georgia old man?"

By now I'd had just about all I could take from this rascal, "no sonny, I got my *own house, and my own land. And my own pocket watch.*"

"Lawd how you talk old man," he said after I showed him my watch. "You musta stold that from a white man, 'cause no negro can afford no watch like it." By now, my anger was really getting out of hand with this youngin's foolishness, and having just about all I could take, I asked him, "so you gonna give me any victuals then?"

He let out a little laugh and said, "naw old man, yo major's gone wait like all de rest of 'em 'til 5. 'Til 5 they gone have to starve I reckon." Not wanting Mister John to have to wait any longer I said, "All right then, I'll tell Mizz Ophelia he'll have to wait." I looked him in the eye when I said this, and if a black man could turn green, then I reckon he just about did. "Wait a minute suh. Do you mean Lead Nurse Miss Ophelia Johnson?"

"That's who I meant, is there more than one of 'em?" His face began to be clearly distorted, and at once he looked contrite & remorseful for his earlier talk. "Ugh…. umm…suh, did she say to say anything if you had to wait 'til 5 to eat?" I was enjoying his change of heart, and while I didn't want him to stew much longer, I simply replied, "indeed suh, that's what she told me."

He didn't let any grass grow under his feet at this point. "SAMMMMMMM, come out heah now!" Shortly after that, a dark man, bigger than the likes of which I ever saw came practically running, and said "yes suh boss, you called me?" Sam's enormous size made two bodies compared to the size of "the boss."

"Yes Sam fix me up a plate of supper loaded to the gills with best of whatever we got back there. Oh, would you like something to eat as well suh?" I hadn't thought about eating in a while, and the more I thought about it, I realized I could eat too. "That's very kind of you, if you could spare a little something for me I'd be most grateful. "Sam make that two of those orders on the double!" "Yes suh boss man, coming up."

As I sat and waited, "the boss" tried his best to stay busy and ignore me 'til Sam came back out with our supper. Next thing I knew, Sam was pushing out a cart with two plates loaded to the gills with country fried steak, mashed potatoes with gravy, corn on the cob, greens, and collards. There was a pitcher of tea with it, and a couple of pieces of lemon meringue pie.

"Thank you Mister Sam, Major Carson and I greatly appreciate it." "My pleasure suh, feel free to come see me whenever y'all be hungry." "Be happy to Mister Sam. Thanks again." As I was pushing the cart out of the mess hall, "the boss" said, "suh, please give my kind regards to Mizz Johnson." "Be happy too. Thanks again." With an irritated look he said, "Anytime suh, anytime."

Inside I smiled, for many years ago Mister Carson told me once, "George, it's not what you know, it's who you know."

'Course he was right, and over the years I'd seen it played out time after time, but it sure was good to see the look on "the bosses" face when I dropped Mizz Ophelia's name on him.

Chapter 14

Back upstairs as I rolled the cart by Mizz Ophelia's desk she asked me if everything went all right down there. "Yes, ma'am, no problem at all. When I mentioned your name to the boss he was most happy to oblige," I said with a smile. She scoffed, then laughed, "Yeah George, I always find Anthony most willing to be of service when he finds out that I requested his service personally," and with that she chuckled. "If you need anything else George, please feel free to give me a holler." "Yes ma'am, thank you again." "My pleasure George."

As I rolled the cart into the room, Mister John woke up from his nap, smelled the plates, and his face lit up instantly. "Bless you George, bless you!" I set his plate, and his tea before him, and watched him eat like a man who hadn't ate in 40 days after being on Mount Sinai with Moses, way back then with all the ancient Israelites.

He noticed a second plate and said, "George, is that for you?"

"Yes suh, when I mentioned to "the boss" down in the mess hall that the Lead Nurse, Miss Ophelia Johnson requested I be taken care of his attitude went from one of a scoundrel, to one of a saint in half a second flat." Mister John chuckled, and then appeared to be slightly in pain. "Mister John, you all right?" "Yeah George, stomach hurts just a little. I'll be fine. Go ahead and eat, otherwise before you know it, you'll turn your back on it, and it'll be gone, 'cause I'm still hungry enough to eat yours too. Go ahead, these gentlemen won't care, and they're passed out anyhow.

"Thank you Mister John, I'm pretty hungry myself." With that, unlike Mister John I took my time. Lawd have mercy! That was the best supper you ever saw. Thank the Lawd my dear Lula can't hear me, 'cause Sam *may* have just topped her delicious cooking. After our early supper Mister John asked the other nurse if he could kindly have the regular supper at 5, and she sweetly replied that they'd be happy to get it for him.

Next morning when I came to see Mister John he was in a decent enough humor. "George, the Doc said he may have to amputate my leg." "Which one, suh,"

I asked. "The right one, he said if they can't stop the infection it'll turn gangrene, and then they'll have to chop it off. I don't want 'em to, but they might not have a choice." Good Lawd, in heaven I thought. "George, would you please send a telegram to Pop and tell him I've been injured, and they may have to cut off my leg please?" "Yes, suh, I will, though you really want to upset him with that, and not just wait to see what happens?" "Naw, 'cause by the time he receives the telegram my leg may already be chopped off." "Lawd have mercy, Mister John. I'll go send it, then come right back to you." "Thanks George, in it give all my love to Susan and the children. See you when you return."

I found the telegraph office, and sent off a telegraph to the Reynolds Telegraph office.

Wednesday September 21, 1864.
10:57 A.M.

To: Mister Joseph J. Carson, eldest son Major John Thomas is in hospital in Lynchburg, VA. Wounded 3X at battle of Winchester, VA. Right leg may have to be amputated. He sends his love to the whole family. Will keep you informed. Your humble servant, George Carson

The next morning a hospital steward had a telegram for me from Reynolds;

Wednesday September 21, 1864. George, thank you for the note. Tell John Thomas we're praying for him. Continue to keep us advised as to the latest. Sincerely, J.J. Carson

I showed Mister John the telegram, and he was glad to see it. About 11 that morning the surgeon came in to see Mister John. "How're you feeling Major?" "Well suh, I feel all right, 'cept my leg is throbbing a little bit." "Your right one?" "Yes suh." "Let me take a look at it Major." The doctor made a whistling sound and called for the nurse. "Nurse, NURSE!!!! Get something to clean this wound again, and rewrap it, *with clean rags this time! How many times do I have to tell y'all to treat our patients with clean bandages?" "But suh, we do the best with what we have, but sometimes it's impossible to have enough clean bandages around here with all the blood and all the bleeding." "Nurse, these men were willing to give it their all for the cause, and they deserve better than that. You know they do. I really don't care if y'all have to stay up all night, every night so we can have fresh bandages around here! Are we clear?" "Yes suh, I understand." "Good, 'cause that'll be a heap big change around here!"*

"Major Carson, I'm sorry to have to tell you this, but, if your leg ain't healed better by morning I'm gonna have to amputate it. I'm terribly sorry Major, but if we don't, then the gangrene will spread throughout your whole body very rapidly, and that will kill you fast. No way to sugarcoat it, so I'm right sorry I might have to do it. Just be prepared for a possible surgery on it first thing in the morning." "Yes suh, Doc, do you have anything to lessen the pain?" Well Major, it breaks my heart to tell, but because of the Yankee blockade of the South, we're well below the minimum levels of medicine we need to take care of our troops. However, I always keep an extra Swoon Bottle for these types of situations, so if your servant George can come with me then he can bring it back to you." "Yes suh, you're most kind, thank you suh."

The surgeon's name was Colonel Jeremiah H. Wilkerson II of Brunswick, GA. He'd been battle surgeon for the Georgia Militia Home Guard for the first two years of the war, but after Gettysburg, a call went out throughout the South for all available Surgeons to be deployed to Virginia immediately. The number of amputations and dead men from disease was spreading like wildfire, but the South's hands were tied behind its back, and medical personnel performed many miracles to save the many brave wounded men, often fighting against two to one odds.

When Doctor Wilkerson took me into his office he told me to shut the door and sit down. "George, where are y'all from?" "Well suh, we're about 5 miles south of Reynolds, GA, residing in Macon County, would the Colonel ever have had reason to go through there?" "The Colonel would. One summer about 6 years ago we went through Reynolds on the way to a family wedding in Columbus. Land sakes alive! I can't tell which was worse, the gnats in Reynolds or the heat in Columbus. 'Course Georgia is known for her heat, but for some reason in Columbus, it always feels *hotter* there than anywhere else in Georgia. Cousin of mine once told me he believes that's because Columbus sits in a bowl, which makes it hotter. I don't rightly know or care, as long as we don't have to visit there in the summertime again."

With that he took his Swoon Bottle out of the desk and poured a little in his coffee cup. He gestured the

bottle towards me, but I said," No, thank you, suh."
"Too early for you, George?" "No suh, I reckon it'd be
nice to have a sip, but I rather Mister John get as much
as he can before you chop off his leg, and I'd rather he
be feeling as little pain as possible."

"Very noble of you George, but don't be concerned
about that. As much as I like Major Carson I can't let it
get out how much my real supply is, or I'd be followed
everywhere I go, night and day 'til the secret got out that
we found a secret stash of Bourbon in the basement of
the hotel as the staff evacuated for the war." With that
he took out another glass and poured a little in the glass
and handed it to me saying, "Don't worry about Major
Carson, George. We got enough of that in the basement
to get the entire hospital, patients and staff feeling no
pain from now, 'til the end of the war, Lord may that
be soon!"

"Now George we know from scripture that the
Apostle Paul said, "And be not drunk with wine, which
is excess; but be filled with the Spirit," in his Epistle to
the Ephesians chapter 5, the 18th verse. But since we are
unable to have any regular medicine due to the blockade,
I'm gonna give you one bottle for Major Carson for
tonight, have him have a large supper, then slowly feed

him the bottle. Make sure he drinks *all of it.* Then in the morning come see me before breakfast, help him have an enormous breakfast, and then feed him the second bottle I'm a gonna give you in the morning. We need him to be passed out during the surgery or be so lickered up and have such a headache that he won't put up any, or much resistance." "Yes suh, I'll do it."

At 5 o'clock I went to pickup Mister John's supper, another superb meal prepared by Sam, Lula her own self would've been proud of it!!! When he was finished eating it, I cleared the room of all dishes and got the bottle.

"George, did the Surgeon get you my medicine for the night?" "Oh, yes suh, have it right here." "Good, 'cause I don't like to take my medicine alone. Perhaps if I must be fed rot gut rye licker, maybe you could "heal thyself," as well." "Well, all right suh, but most of this "medicine" is for you, Surgeon's orders." "All right, George, if you insist." I grabbed two glasses and poured a healthy amount into Mister John's and a very small measure in mine.

Mister John needs this much more than I do tonight, since it's his last night on earth with his right leg and all I 'spose. "To the Confederacy, may she survive to fight another day." With that we clincked glasses. "Good Lord

George, this ain't rot gut at all. This is the finest Bourbon you ever saw. I've never ever had any better than this before." I tasted some too, and he was right. At least his "medicine" went down smooth. For the next few hours, Mister John and I reminisced about all the good times we had when he and his brothers were growing up.

"George, you remember the time James and I tried to get Bess to go swimming with us, and she wasn't having nothing of it. Then James and I decided to light her tail on fire to get her in? Well, she went in all right." Mister John laughed, and laughed, and laughed. When he was done, he coughed a little, but he didn't appear too bad off in his lungs. "George, I never saw you so mad before in my life! Before or after, and that was over 25 years ago, George, surely you've laughed about it since then, if'n even in private?" I laughed a loud belly laugh, not worried about the other officers in the room, 'cause they were practically always asleep, and the only time they woke up was to eat. "Yes suh, I've laughed many, many times over that over the years, but ole Bess never thought it was funny I'm sure." Mister John thought that was hilarious. I reckon since we were into our second hour of his medicine, he was already feeling no pain.

"George, nobody likes to take their medicine alone, have a little, will you? I appreciate your concern for my health, but I reckon there's plenty in there." So I poured a little bit more, not much though, for I needed to keep my head clear for my ministrations. Lawd that stuff was good! I couldn't wait to get back home and have some at Carson House with Mister Carson, and smoke our pipes, and forget this nonsense ever occurred!

"Mister John, how's your leg feel?" "George, I'll be honest with you, it hurts! Although, "my medicine" is helping that quite a bit. George, be honest with me.

You reckon Culnel Wilkerson is going to chop off my leg in the morning? Is that what the swoon bottle is for? I mean, I ain't complaining or anything." "Suh, I reckon he said it was *in case* they had to do that. In the morning if he thinks it's all right, he won't do it. However, if he intends to chop it off, then we'll do this all over again in the morning so you won't be feeling any pain, suh. He said your head might feel like the ocean's pounding against it if'n you don't fall asleep, but you'll be easier for us to hold during the surgery. Mister John, I pray the good Lawd will heal your leg suh, I really do."

Mister John was quiet for a long moment thinking about what the next 12 hours would bring. "Thank you ever so much, dear George, may Providence reward your kindness to me. If the good Lord wants my leg, it's his to take. "Thou giveth, and thou taketh away. Blessed be thy name, oh Lord." We just sat there for a while, Mister John silently consuming his medicine, me thinking of ways to cheer him up.

"Suh, there's a heap of veterans who're missing arms and legs from this blasted war. Least you're still alive don't that count for something?" "Yes George, I reckon it counts for a whole lot. The Yankees might've taken my leg, but they can't take my spirit. George, my medicine is working fine. I can't keep my eyes open much longer. Thank ever so kindly for your ministrations of my medicine. Good night." "Good night, Mister John. Sleep tight young man."

We all got a good night sleep, and I was up early checking on Mister John. He said his head didn't really hurt too bad, but his leg did. Oh dear Lawd have mercy, please Father don't bring any more misery on your servants Mister Carson and all his family. Mister John had a breakfast fit for a King!

Three eggs sunny side up, a big piece of ham steak, cheese grits with gravy on top, and biscuits with gravy on 'em. Truth be told, his portions were two to three times larger than the other poor soldiers breakfasts, but whenever I went to the mess hall to pick up our meals, "the boss" never said a word to me when I picked up our food from Mister Sam. "Thank you so much Mister Sam! If anyone ever doubted in heaven, all they'd have to do is eat your fine cooking and they'd believe!" "Thank you Mista George, you're most kind suh. My regards to Mista Carson." "I'll do it Sam, thank you." Mister Sam prepared the same meal for me, bless his heart, and again "the boss" saw it, but he quickly looked away.

Mister John and I enjoyed our breakfast mostly in silence, even though we didn't have to, since the other officers in the room were sleeping the sleep of the dead. After I cleared out all the plates and such, the Surgeon came to see Mister John. "Good morning, Suh." "Good morning, George, 'tis indeed a beautiful day outside, not too hot, not too cold, just right. Morning, Major. How ya feeling this fine day?" "Suh I'm all right, but to be honest with you my leg don't feel right. Throbs all the time and all. Although, it felt a lot better last night with "my medicine." Thank you ever so kindly for it." Colonel Wilkerson smirked a half smile, and said "let me have a look at it." He pulled the bed sheet off it, and Lawd have mercy, land sakes alive was that the worst smell I've ever smelt. It took of the Surgeon's will power to keep his face straight. "Nurse, clean this wound up, and prepare for surgery. Major Carson suh, it gives me no pleasure to tell you that I'm gonna have to take that leg off below the knee before it becomes infected anymore. We have zero medicine to heal that wound if it spreads any further. I'll be back in 3 hours sharp for surgery. Good day, suh. George, would you kindly come with me?"

"Yes, suh." We walked back to his office, and he shut the door. "Dear Lord in heaven George! You knew we're gonna have to operate didn't you?" "Yes suh, it looked, and *smelled* something awful! How in the world did the sheets hold back that smell suh?" "I don't know, George, never studied how that happens. Here's what we're gonna do." He reached down into his desk like he did yesterday and produced another Swoon Bottom, which looked the same as the one from yesterday.

"Same procedure George, you've got 3 hours for him to consume this entire bottle. Don't worry it won't kill him if the gangrene does not first. None for you! I assume he asked you to have a little of his "medicine" with him last night, and you did, but very little. How am I doing so far?" "Yes suh, that's pretty much how it happened." "Don't worry, George, this ain't the first time I've had to treat our brave soldiers with "alternative medicines." This one is a proof slightly higher than the other. When he wakes up *he will* have a headache for sure, but the nurses can treat that, and hopefully we can stop the spread of gangrene in time. Thank you ever so kindly for your Christian heart, and for being such a good *friend* to Major Carson."

Reckon now wasn't the time to start crying and all, so I said, "Yes suh, thank you, suh. I'll make sure he's ready for you in 3 hours." "Very good, George, see you then." When I got back to the hospital room, Mister John saw me with the bottle, and he was a good sport about it. "George, when we get back to the great state of Georgia, you reckon you'd make me a Pegleg like so many of our other soldiers have now?" "Indeed suh, be happy to. You want a pine one, or an oak one?" "Aw come now George. You're just playing with me right? Everybody knows a pine tree ain't worth a lick. Oak or cedar would be much better." I laughed, and he did too. "You knew I was just pulling your chain, did you suh? 'Course I'll make it outta oak, or cedar.

Everyone in Macon County knows Mister Carson wouldn't have a pine tree at his house, for fear of it blowing over when the wind blows slightly faster than normal." He laughed, and I was glad. Mister John is a smart fella, reckon that's why they gave him command of Company C, 'cause he's got a good head on his shoulders. I got his glass from last night and poured it almost to the top. He noticed this and said, "I know what we're doing here, George, but we do indeed have 3 hours to prepare for surgery." "Surgeon's orders suh, just doing my job." He smiled at that, and laughed, "In the last 3 years, George, the well of licker has practically been dry, and in the last 15 hours the floodgates seem to be flowing freely with it." I laughed as he tasted his first sip.

"George, you might recall from last night, but a gentleman doesn't prefer to have "his medicine" alone. You may want to write that down somewhere." We both chuckled at that. "Well suh, the offer's quite tempting, but the Surgeon said, "George, this morning the patient is to consume all of his *medicine alone*. Let me let you in on a little secret, Mister John." "Fire away, George." "As you may notice suh, the Surgeon does indeed have more than one Swoon Bottle." "Indeed, that thought just crossed my mind." "Well suh, it seems that when they were converting this former resort into a hospital,

Colonel Wilkerson and his staff found so much bourbon in the basement, that he said it 'would keep the entire hospital, patients and staff feeling no pain 'til the end of the war.'" Mister John laughed hysterically at that one, so I said, "Suh, after your Surgery, Colonel Wilkerson said you're gonna have a mighty big headache, but the nurses can help with that. After that, if you're feeling up to it, maybe the Surgeon would be kind enough to share some more "medicine." He laughed, it was 11:00, one more hour 'til the surgery, and he was feeling no pain. "George, I'd certainly like that. In the meantime woul..d you po me notha, p..p...please?" "Yes suh, I reckon you got two more glasses left then you'll be done with the bottle." Thnk GGGorge, you..ways re..nce to m." He put his head down for a second, then chugged the entire glass with one gulp. "WHEEEEEEEEEEEE!

George, I'm flying George, I'm flying. May I hve notha ggg..lss pls?" "Yes suh, coming right up." I handed him the last glass, and he chugged half of it, and fell back in his bed. "George, the room's spinning. George!!!! There's three of you. You gggot ootthr brohts?" "No Mister John, I'm right here in the middle you see me now?" "Yyyye Ge.. I se...yo. Could I have so mo... "me...ine pplse?" "Here Mister John, drink all of it!"

"Thx Gggge...," and he finished the rest of the glass. When he did, his eyes got as bright as the stars, and then I quickly grabbed the glass as he closed his eyes, and fell back into his bed stone drunk. Not a thing in this universe was gonna wake that poor gentleman up, 'cept maybe sawing off his leg. The Surgeon came in shortly after he took his final sip with an envoy of 6 orderlies, and 4 nurses. "Is he dead, Doctor?" Inquired lead nurse Mizz Ophelia Johnson. "No ma'am, he's heavily intoxicated," he said winking at me, and said, "However, it's my experience that when I make my first deep cut the patient will awake quite violently, that's why you orderlies are here. One of you will hold down each extremity, one will hold his head, and another will hold a bit in his mouth. George, would you kindly hold the bit in his mouth?" "Yes suh, be glad to." After he put the tourniquet over his femoral artery on his right thigh, the surgeon said, "All right ladies and gentlemen, this is it. Hold on. Patients in surgery for amputation can exhibit the strength of an ox initially, before they give up, so hold on real tight. It's important that you keep him as still as possible." Mister John had one an orderly holding down each of his feet, one on each arm. A very large man holding down his head, and I held down the bit in his mouth from underneath the bed. This was the best spot I thought for the best angle to use all of my strength. After I wrapped the ropes around both of my wrists, I secured them in my palms and pulled taught, but not all the way until, or if he woke up.

Colonel Wilkerson stood on Mister John's right side, and then announced, "Here we go. Hang on gentlemen, and he placed his scalpel barely above his right knee. He cut in a circular motion, and got Mizz Johnson to hold on to the loose skin two or three inches above the knee. Everything was going smoothly until the Surgeon cut into his nerves, and that woke up Mister John in no time flat. The reins in my hand became taut instantly, and though the good Lawd's allowed me to retain my strength in my old age, was he testing me now to see if I'd taken care of his temple? Perhaps, but I was holding on for dear life, as were the other 5 on his arms and legs. The big man didn't look like he was having any trouble, but that's 'cause he'd done this many times, and while he was strong as an ox, it took all his might to at least not look like he was using any effort at all. Coming out behind the bit were words I thought might've been ones spoken when there were no ladies and gentlemen were around, the likes of which scamps dared to use. I was thankful for the bit since the nurses were there, and didn't want their ears to be polluted by Mister John's colorful choice of words. He thrusted like an animal up and down, his eyes became big as saucers, and snot was running out of his nose. He kept up his thrashing for a good 5 minutes while Colonel Wilkerson kept cutting like he was the only one in the room, focused only his cutting. Exactly 5 minutes after he woke up and starting thrashing violently, his eyes became even bigger than saucers, he bucked his head up as far as he could push the big man's hands, then closed his eyes and fell limp back to his bed.

Chapter 15

" **N**ice work gentlemen, he'll be out for hours now. And after I sew him back up, nurses, you can check up on him every now and then to comfort him." Everybody breathed a sigh of relief. Thank heaven there were so many of us to hold him down, because with so many of us applying pressure on his body it wore him out much faster than it would've worn out one or two men trying to hold him down. Before the war Mister John stood head to head with me, and the Doctor told me I'm 5 feet, 10 inches tall.

Mister John weighed 195 pounds before the war, (thanks no doubt to my baby's spectacular cooking), before he was shot I'd say he must've been 160 lbs. soaking wet, for the shortage of food in the South had decimated the South almost as bad as the Yankees had. All the men in Company C had lost lots of weight in the last three years. Their well meaning families back home wanted to send some food to their hero's, but didn't have enough for themselves, much less their hero's. So, the brave men made do on whatever they could find. If you would've told these men 10, even 5 years ago that in 5 years from now they'd be starving, and constantly trying to find some nourishment from whatever source they could, they'd laughed you out of the house. Back then, nobody was hungry, and today everybody was. Thus, I wondered if Mister John was back at his prewar weight of 195 lbs., how long he could've held out against us.

When Colonel Wilkerson was done with surgery he had the nurses cleaned up the blood, and all the mess from the surgery, he had the nurses' change his sheets, and had me and another nurse watching him around the clock to make sure he didn't go into shock.

He woke up the next morning at 7:00 o'clock with a headache, the pounding of which he said he didn't wish on his worst enemies, *"even the Yankees."* Nurse Johnson had kindly volunteered to take the night watch, while she provided a cot for me in the hallway since there wasn't any room for it in the room. "Good morning, Major Carson," she said. At first Mister John was happy to see a pretty face the likes of which he hadn't seen that fine since he first met his future wife Mizz Susan Saphronia Howe more than 17 years ago. "Good morning, ma'am," he replied with a smile until he remembered the drums banging in his head like fireworks on New Year's Eve. She put some balm on his chapped lips and had him sit up and drink 5 cups of water before she allowed him to speak. When he was finished, she asked him if he felt better, and he replied, "Much." Then he looked down at his leg and remembered why he was here.

He told her his right foot itched, and she looked at him compassionately and told him that they had taken it off at the knee yesterday, but it was normal to feel what the surgeon called a "Phantom Itch." "Are you hungry, Major," she asked him, and he said he was so hungry he could eat a horse.

I was there when he woke up and glad he appeared to getting along fine. "George, Honey, could you go down to the mess and tell Mister Sam to prepare three plates of breakfast for me, with three pitchers each of water, orange juice, and coffee?" "Yes ma'am, I'll be right back." "Thank you, George." Mizz Johnson was so sweet. I surely hoped she got a fine Christian husband soon after this war was over, and they'd never have to live through the devastation this one had caused ever again.

When I got down to the mess hall, "the boss" was at the front door helping the walking wounded find a table to sit at and make sure they got enough to eat, until he could hurry 'em out and allow the rest of the ambulatory patients to have breakfast. Those bedridden were served first by order of the Surgeon General Samuel Preston Moore MD CSA on his last visit through the hospital, because he was appalled that those well enough to walk were able to go to the mess hall and eat up all the food before the weakest among 'em were able to get any victuals. Surgeon General Moore had screamed at Colonel Wilkerson, the head Surgeon, who in turn had screamed at Lead Nurse Mizz Ophelia Johnson, who had in turn screamed at "the boss" that anybody who got caught eating so much as a thimble full of food before the bedridden patients had eaten would certainly be hung before the entire hospital on a set of 50 feet gallows, along with whoever served 'em. Now this was mainly due to two things.

First, at the time of Surgeon General Moore's visit there was an extreme food shortage and through the valor of brave rebel soldiers going behind enemy lines at night there was just enough food for every patient in the hospital. The problem was that when the ambulatory ate their meals which were enough to sustain 'em 'til the next meal, most were still slightly hungry because of their deprivation of the last three years, and thus the still hungry soldiers would bribe the staff with worthless Confederate dollars, who didn't know the difference, and thus created a shortage for the bedridden. With the stocks full for the moment, technically Mizz Johnson didn't violate Surgeon General Moore's order when she told me to go down there and get some supper for Mister Carson that first day we were here, if not violating the spirit of the law. Mizz Johnson knew there was plenty of food in the pantry that day, and as far as she was concerned she had violated no orders.

Meanwhile, when "the boss" saw me he yelled, "Saaaaam!" He came trotting out and said, "King George is here Sam," and with that he walked off. That was cute. King George huh? "Good morning, Mister Sam." "Good morning, Mista George, how can I help you suh?" "Mister Sam, would you be so kind to make three of those most delicious *breakfasts* you made for us yesterday please, suh?" "Yes suh, be more'n happy to, Mista George. Coming right up!!!" It didn't take Sam no time at all to whip up our breakfasts, and by the time I got back to

Mister John's room, I could practically hear his stomach growl from outside the room. "Why thank you George, that was fast," said Mizz Johnson. "Yesum, Mister Sam takes good care of me." I carried Mister John's tray over to him and poured him some coffee. "Bless you, George, and please tell Mister Sam his cooking is just about as amazing as your lovely wife's. Also, before I forget, could you send the family a telegram after breakfast with the news of my surgery, but let 'em know that other than that I'm fine?" "Yes, suh, be happy too."

Mizz Johnson was woofing her grits and gravy down faster than I'd ever seen, certainly much faster than a lady ought to eat. I was trying not to stare but couldn't help it. After shoving an enormous amount of grits, biscuit, and sausage in her mouth, she chewed it feverishly and swallowed. "Pardon my manners, Major, and George. My first day here I learned quick that when one gets a spare moment to eat while on shift here *to take it!*" "It's quite all right Mizz Johnson you don't have to explain that to us. George and I have been living like that for over 3 years now. Eat when you can, sleep when you can, do whatever you need to do when you can," said Mister John. "Why thank you, kind suh, you are ever such an understanding gentleman."

"Miss Johnson may I inquire as to your date of birth ma'am?" "Certainly, suh, I was born on Thursday, April 2nd, in 1846. May I inquire why you're interested since I see by your ring you're a married man?" "Huh, oh, no I wasn't asking for myself ma'am if that's what you thought. Hey, wait a minute, you said you were born on April 2nd, 1846?" "Yes suh, that's the day my mother delivered me at our home, just south of Richmond." "That's my younger brother Bob's birthday, which is in fact the reason I was asking how old you are. Y'all are exactly the same age! Would you mind Miss Johnson if I introduced y'all someday?" "Major, if he's in any way like you, then I'd be delighted to meet him." "Thank you, ma'am, Bob will be delighted to know you I'm sure."

After breakfast I went to send Mister Carson and Mizz Susan a telegram letting 'em know about Mister John's surgery.

Sunday September 25, 1864
Lynchburg, VA

Dear Mister Carson and Miss Susan, it is with great regret that I must tell you the head Surgeon for the hospital, Colonel Wilkerson,

> *had to amputate Mister John's right leg at the knee. He is recovering well, and sends his love. Your humble servant, George Carson*

Mister Carson took the news about as well as one would expect a father to take the news of his son's leg being amputated. Both he and Mizz Susan were at least grateful he was still alive. They were hoping that Mister John and his two brothers would be home soon, and this horrible war would soon be over before it destroyed the South.

On Monday Colonel Wilkerson came in after breakfast to check on Mister John. "Good morning Major, how are you this fine day?" "Suh, I've never felt better. If'n I could go back and be with my men I'd leave right now." "Well, Major, unfortunately I'm not sure when, or if you're ever going back to your men. We've got to make sure your leg heals correctly first. We need to make sure it doesn't get infected before we let you go back to the fight Major." "Yes suh, I understand. Thank you for your kind treatment of me." "How's the leg feel, Major?" "Well, I reckon it feels all right, but sometimes it feels like it's still there, like it was before you cut it off. Suh, it's a strange feeling." "Don't worry, son, it happens more often than not when a soldier gets an appendage amputated, there's often a ghost feeling for a while of the severed limb, nothing unusual about it. Well, everything looks all right. I'll see you tomorrow morning. Good day, Major. Miss Johnson may I see you in private please ma'am?" The doctor waited for Mizz Johnson to step outside, and then he followed her.

When they were in his office in private, he shut the door, and then sat down at his desk. "Miss Johnson, are you all right? Are you getting enough rest?" "Yes suh, I'm all right. I get enough sleep at night. Sometimes I have nightmares of all the horrors the Yankees have caused our poor, brave men like Major Carson." "Yes ma'am, I know what you mean. Anyway, the reason I wanted to talk to you in private is that after amputations there is a high probability that the area which was severed can get infected with disease, which may cause a rather quick and painful death for which we have no medicines to treat the Major with because of the blockade. So, what I need you to do is keep your eye on it and clean it regularly with clean water, soap, and clean rags. Also, tell the nurse who relieves your shift this and make sure she tells her relief this as well." "Yes suh, I'll make sure they all know how to treat that poor man." "Thank you

Miss Johnson, now if you'll excuse me, ma'am, I have to catch up on my paperwork."

During the day, Mister John and I played cards, read old newspapers, discarded books left behind by other patients, whatever we could get our hands on. I asked Mizz Johnson if I could smoke my pipe, and she said that was fine but asked me to open the window. Actually after lunch when we were out in the hall she told me to smoke it all the time if I could, for not only did it smell aromatic, but it helped block some of the horrible smells of the poor suffering men whom they were unable to treat with modern medicines.

I asked Mister John how he felt the next morning, and he said he felt all right. His leg hurt a little mainly he said he was glad the pounding in his head was gone from consuming both of those Swoon Bottles in a 15 hour period. He said it felt like somebody was pounding on his head with a sledge hammer all day Saturday, and all day Sunday. "Now that I'm clear headed, George, I feel much, much better. Hopefully when you get my pegleg made up, I'll be able to get around same as I used to before." "Yes suh, that'll be real nice. Soon as we get home for your recovery I'll make you one up." "Thank you George, it'll be good to be home finally. I reckon they won't need me in the Army anymore.

There's lots of soldiers fighting without arms, but I haven't seen any that I remember without a leg that they let stay in for long after it happened."

"Yes suh, reckon you're right about that. Can't say that I recall too many, or *any* one legged soldiers fighting for long after they've had the surgery. Mister John, do you recall that time when that 200 lb. buck was headed straight for Mister James and me, and you spared us from becoming mincemeat?" Mister John chuckled, "I'll never forget that day, George! Every time I ever shot a Yankee I imagined him charging at us like that big buck. Lord have mercy!!! You reckon James made a mess in his britches that day?" I laughed and laughed and laughed. I almost was worried about waking the other patients in the room, but then I remembered they probably wouldn't wake up if'n a cannonball landed in the room, and then I was laughing so hard tears started rolling out of my eyes.

"I don't recall now whether he did or he didn't. Although, I do remember him being so frightened and shook up, that he *probably* made a mess in his britches. That was one great shot you made, Mister John. Didn't you shoot that beast in his right eye?" Mister John thought about it, "I can't really remember, George. I thought it might've been in the head, all I know is that he was some good eating huh? I'll never forget that venison Miss Lula whipped up for us. I don't remember anyone in the family who didn't have seconds of that stew she made! I can't wait to see that wonderful wife of yours, George! Although Mister Sam does run a close second to her I reckon, but I'll never tell her, lessen I want to get slapped." I laughed out loud again, "Yes suh, that's it. Stay out of that woman's way, lessen you wanna get run over like that buck almost did to us."

The next morning on Wednesday, September 28th Colonel Wilkerson came in the room with a smile and a dapper mood. "Good morning, Major Carson, how's your leg feeling?" "Good morning, suh, it aches a little, reckon that's pretty normal though." "Yes and no. Let me take a look at it."

The Surgeon undid the fresh wrappings, and when he saw his stump of a knee he made the slightest wrinkle around his eyes that 9 out of 10 men wouldn't have noticed. But I did. "Miss Johnson, when was the last time you cleaned his stump, and changed his dressings?" "About 30 minutes ago, suh. Is everything all right?"

"Yes, yes, everything's fine. Major, if you have no more problems today I'll see you again in the morning. Good day." With that, he hustled out of the room, on the way to the next patient on his rounds.

When Mizz Johnson stepped out of the room, I asked her if everything was okay with Mister John, and she said he was fine, but the surgeon is really concerned about the leg being infected with disease since they didn't have any medicine to treat it. I told her thank you, and begged off.

After lunch, Mister John said he didn't feel well. Mizz Johnson asked him what was wrong, and he said he had a headache. She suggested he take a nap, and so he did. He slept most of the afternoon, and was only up long enough after that to eat supper, and then he slept straight through the night 'til 7:00 O'clock the next morning. Mister John woke up covered in sweat, and the nurse felt his forehead and she said his head was real hot to the touch, but he was shivering and said he was really cold. Mizz Johnson went and got the Surgeon two hours ahead of his rounds. As soon as he got there his suspicions from yesterday were confirmed, the leg had become infected, the infection had spread throughout the entire body, and the hospital didn't have any way of treating him, other than basic treatment of the sick that

217

anybody knew how to give. The nurses brought more blankets, and applied cold wet towels to his forehead to try and cool him down. When the surgeon was done with his visit he asked to see me in the hall. "George, I'm very sorry to have to tell you this, but Major Carson's leg has been infected, and it looks like the infection has spread throughout his entire body. Today's Thursday, if he makes it to Saturday, I'll be shocked. Because of the blockade we don't have any medicine to try and stop the infection.

It kills me a little inside every time I see brave men like Major Carson suffer, and we have no way of treating 'em properly." He put his hands on both of my shoulders and looked me right in the eyes. George, you've been a huge help to Major Carson these last three years, and I can tell y'all have a great relationship. George, when the good Lord says his time is up I want you to take him home to Reynolds. I've got a horse and buggy out back you can borrow, and if I'm ever up in Macon County after the war I'll come and get it. If not, consider it yours 'til then." He pulled out two handfuls of confederate dollars and handed them to me. "These won't get you too much but take 'em. Somebody will want 'em." Then he pulled out a $50 dollar Shinplaster and said, "Here you go, George. This should help you get back home without any troubles." I looked him in the eyes with shock. He didn't really know me, and I didn't know him, and here he was showing me some of the finest southern hospitality you ever saw. "Why I don't know what to say suh, I reckon I'll just say thank you from the bottom of my heart." "No need, George, but thank you. You're been a huge help to Major Carson, and a brave young officer such as he deserves to be buried in his own land around his own people. Not in some veterans cemetery in Lynchburg, VA with men he might've never known." "No, suh, when the good Lawd takes him to glory, I'll take him home and make sure he's buried next to his brother in the Bryan-Carson cemetery." "All right, George, I'll come back in a few hours to check on him. In the meantime the nurses will take real good care of him to try as best they can to manage his pain. If he's not in too much pain maybe y'all could talk about old times when he was growing up. That'll take his mind of his situation. It is truly amazing how the brain can if not heal people with positive thinking, it can certainly act as a balm in lessening the pain." "Yes suh, you're most kind, and I'll be sure to tell his father, Mister Carson of your kindness, 'cause I'm sure he'll be very happy to hear of it. Good day, suh." "Good day, George."

I went back in the room, and Mister John looked a little better, but not much. The nurses were comforting him as best as they could. After breakfast, the nurses were trying their hardest to get the fever down but said it was a losing effort. Around 11 in the morning, Mizz Johnson asked me to step out in the hall, and what was right in front of my eyes, but none other than Mister Joseph, and MisterRobert. "George!" said Mister Robert, and ran up and gave me a hug. I tried to shake Mister Joseph's hand, but he too gave me the biggest bear hug I ever had. Luckily he didn't crush any of these old bones of mine.

"We came as soon as we could, George. They even said we could come back tomorrow should need be," said Mister Joseph. "How is he, George? Is he gonna be all right?" "Not sure, Mister Bob, the Surgeon, Colonel Wilkerson said he'd be shocked if he lived 'til Saturday because of the infection in his leg." "Dear Lord! He didn't give him no chance at all then?" "No, Mister Bob, I reckon he didn't." "This is gonna break Pop's heart. First James, and then then John, this is gonna tear him up mighty big." "We know, Bob," said Mister Joe.

"George, how did he get injured?" "Well, Mister Joe, I reckon the Yankees shot him in the arm in the morning, but it didn't really hurt nothing. And then he went back in the fighting, and they was a fighting something fierce, and he got shot in the leg on the retreat, but right after that I think they shot him in the stomach. His men carried him outta there, which was very kind of 'em since the Yankees were raining bullets down on 'em like flies on a hawg on a hot summer day. Anyhow, we were able to make it here to Lynchburg, VA last week. They chopped off his leg the other day, and then it became infected, and then heaven blessed us with your presence. He'll be so glad to see y'all he won't know what to do!"

"George, we haven't eaten in a day and a half. And that was just some victuals we scrounged from some Yankees who ran from us. They were mighty good, just not enough.

Where can we find something to eat in this place?" I took out my pocket watch to check the time, 11:09 hmmmm, "Mister Joe, if you go down to the first floor, then make a right and go yonder all the way to the end of the building you'll see the mess hall. If you run into a crazy freed black man they call "the boss," tell him y'all want some lunch, and when he gets into a tizzy about lunch not being served 'til noon, then play along with him for a little bit, and tell him y'all hadn't eaten in a while. He'll say he don't care, lunch is at noon, "come back then." So when he says that tell him, "Fine. I'll tell Lead Nurse Mizz Ophelia Johnson she'll have to wait 'til 12:00 O'clock for us to eat."

I was in the hallway when they came back, bellies full, and smiling like they'd just heard a funny joke or something. "George, that was some of the best cooking I ever had this side of Lula's kitchen," said Robert. Joe said, "We did what you said George, and you shoulda seen the look on "the bosses" face when we were about to leave and said, 'Fine. I'll tell Lead Nurse Ophelia Johnson she'll have to wait 'til 12:00 O'clock for us to eat." He looked so mad he could chew nails and spit fire. Anyhow, next thing we know he yells, '*SSSSSSS-SAAAAAAAAAAAAAAAAAMMMMMMM!!!!!!!!!!!!*' And this big fella came out of the kitchen, nice as he could be and took our orders, and in no time flat our food was ready, and Bob's right. It was indeed some of the best cooking we've ever had outside of your lovely wife's kitchen. We took our lunch in the mess, and when we left "the boss" wouldn't even look at us." I laughed, and so did the boys. I still thought of 'em as boys, even though now they're both men fighting in a war that was about to kill half of their brothers who enlisted in it. Lawd have mercy.

"I told Mister John y'all are here, and he's glad to see you. He looks sort of weak, so don't go getting him excited, Mister Bob, you hear?" "Yes, George, I won't." "Good, now y'all can go right in. Oh, one more thing. There's other officers in there, but they're asleep. Been so the whole time he's been in there, so don't mind 'em."

With that they went into the room, Mister Joe first, followed by Mister Bob. Mister John looked a lot better than the last time I'd seen him, so I immediately suspected Colonel Wilkerson's Swoon Bottle, but couldn't be sure. "Joe, Bob, y'all come on in ya hear? How y'all doing?" "We're doing great brother, when are they discharging you so you can get back into the fight?" Joe replied for the both of 'em. "I don't rightly know brother. To be honest with you, I can't say as I know. The Colonel said my leg has become infected, and he's trying his best to treat it, but without medicine because of the blockade he feels like his hands are tied behind his back." I was wondering how he had improved so quickly.

My suspicions were confirmed when he told 'em how "the good Cunnel has left me some "medicine" for the pain though, which is helping me immensely."

Mister John's bed was against the wall, and when I saw the evidence on the floor between the bed and the wall, I knew Colonel Wilkerson had indeed slipped Mister John some more medicine. Although there was no need to consume near the amounts he'd had the other day and night, since they weren't gonna chop off any more appendages.

"Bob, look at you boy, are you staying out of trouble?" "Yes, suh, I am, a fella can't get in no trouble being a courier for General Dole and General Cook. No suh, I haven't been up to any devilment...*yet.*" "Now looky heah son, the war is almost over. We've fought the Yankees with everything we've had and then some. But there's too many of 'em, too many guns, too many canons, too may artillery shells, *TOO MANY YANKEES!!!* Now the best thing we can do is fight 'til we can't fight anymore, which I suspect will be in much less than a year. You will stay alive Bob for Pop. Being a courier ain't a very glorious job I know, but *it will keep you alive boy.* Now, Captain Joe P. Carson look at you and look at that fancy Whitworth rifle would you? May I see it?" Mister Joe gladly handed it to his older brother who handled it with care. "How far you reckon this beauty will fire up to, Joe?"

"Well, they say up to 1800 yards, but nobody's quite sure. This past May at the Battle of Spotsylvania Courthouse, one of my men hit that Yankee General Sedgwick from 1,200 yards. Sergeant E. R. Grace was the one who shot him in the head, and later he told me he could've easily hit him from 1,800 yards. Some of my men later heard that the Yankees were hunkered down in their ditches, taking cover from our rifles, and that buffoon Yankee General was heard taunting his men saying, "Those Johnny Rebels can't hit us up here men..," and when the words were coming out of his mouth, Sergeant Grace's head shot took him out."

"Well I declare, too bad we couldn't have had these rifles for all the men from the beginning, and not just for your Sharpshooters." "Well, they say the folks in Richmond can't afford to outfit the entire South with 'em because it'd be too expensive, John, besides, these rifles are great for long distance shooting, but they ain't for fighting in real close, 'cause once you fire 'em they're real hard to reload. Takes a lot of practice, and your average infantry trooper would be better off with a standard rifle, than a Whitworth." "Very impressive, Joe! Gentlemen, it's such a pleasure to see y'all again. Too bad it's not under better circumstances. I feel I must take a nap to regain my strength, would y'all kindly excuse me for a while?" "'Course we can, brother," said Bob proudly. "We'll come back later, John, when you've refreshed yourself," Mister Joe told him.

Mister John slept most of the afternoon, while Mizz Johnson and her assistant made sure he was taken care of. His temperature was said to have dropped by Mizz Johnson's assistant, Nurse Luwanda. It was a bright sunny day, without a cloud in the sky, so Mister Joe, Mister Bob, and I decided to go out and get some fresh air.

"George, he don't look good," said Bob. "I know, Mister Bob, he ain't even 40 years old now and looks to be as old as I am. Lawd have mercy!

Mister Joe, how'd you get so lucky to make it through this war without a scratch so far?" He scratched his head and thought for a second. "I reckon it's 'cause the good Lord looks after his children when they seek him with all their heart. Some of my men say some of them Yankees don't even believe in the good Lord, and his heaven and all that. But let me tell you George, when those men are down in the trenches trying to blow each others heads off with their rifles, their canons, and their artillery, *every single cotton picking one of 'em believes in the good Lord. North and South. Yes suh, that's a fact!"* After mulling this over for a while I reckoned he was right. Sometimes folks don't pray as much as they should, and read their scriptures like they ought too, but when someone was trying to kill 'em, *they all believed.*

"George, hopefully John Thomas will recover, but if he's been infected by some bug in that hospital he'll be gone in no time. Seen it happen too many times in the last few years. None of my men wanna get anywhere near a hospital, for they know it's only a matter of time before they meet their maker, and they'd much rather take a Yankee bullet in the head. John's putting up a good fight for our behalf, but I can tell it's everything he has just to appear pleasant. We'll go calling on him after supper tonight, and after breakfast in the morning, then we've gotta get back to the 4th Georgia Regiment. Otherwise they'll be saying we went AWOL or some such nonsense." "That sounds good Mister Joe. When his time is up, and the good Lawd recalls him unto his glory I'll take him back to Georgia so your father may burry him. Colonel Wilkerson let me borrow his horse and wagon and gave me a little money for the trip." He reached for his wallet and handed me some money, "Here, George, take some more. This Confederate money ain't hardly worth the paper it's printed on, but it might get ya something." "That's very kind of you, Mister Joe, if you insist." "Afraid so, George, I want our brother to be taken home with the dignity he deserves and not buried in some veterans cemetery in Ole Virginny, where neither Pop and Susan, nor John's children will have any closure of his memory.

George, would you pass on to Pop and Miss Susan our condolences, and tell 'em how sorry we are about all this. Tell 'em I'll do my darndest to make sure neither Bob nor I come home like that." "Yes suh, I'd be happy to. Now speaking of that, I wanna see y'all alive too, so after the war we can put all this behind us as one big unhappy memory." I took out my pipe, and Mister Joe took out a cigar as we relaxed in the warm but not too hot sun. Thank the Lawd summer had finally passed, and autumn was here with its warm days, and cool nights. Maybe it was a way the good Lawd lets you know he loves you 'cause he replaces the brutally hot Southern summers with gentle breezy days, soon abounding with falling leaves, and pretty soon frost on the ground in the middle of November. Yes suh, I'm old enough to know the seasons now like clockwork. Even in Virginia, the weather seemed to be about the same as it was back home in Georgia. 'Cept Ole Virginny was definitely colder in the winter! And she was hot in summertime, but not quite as hot as Reynolds. One good thing I loved about Ole Virginny was that she didn't have any gnats! Thank you dear Lawd in heaven for that!

After supper, Mister Joe, Mister Bob, and myself went in to see Mister John. He was awake when we went in, and didn't see us at first, but we could see him. He appeared to be in a lot of pain, but when Mister Joe said "Hello, John," he immediately smiled, and said, "Well, look what the cat dragged in." Each brother took his time hugging Mister John, and when they were done I could've sworn I saw a tear in his eye but next thing I knew it wasn't there. Either way, it was emotional for all three brothers, for everybody knew what each other was thinking, but nobody was willing to say anything, so nobody said nothing. Finally Mister John said, "Sounds like a Quaker meeting in here." They laughed, and then Mister Joe said Bob and he were here for a quick visit and then would stop by in the morning before they had to report back to the 4th Georgia Regiment.

John said it was too bad they had to leave tomorrow, and they agreed. "Well, we'll see you in the morning brother. Get a good night's sleep now, ya hear?" "Yes suh!" Mister John sounded off to his lower ranking younger sibling. "Good night gentlemen!"

Out in the hall I thanked 'em for coming, wished 'em a good night, and said we looked forward to seeing 'em in the morning. After breakfast in the Mess Hall with all the other sick and wounded the next morning we headed up to Mister John's room. When we walked into the room we froze, for the Surgeon, Colonel Wilkerson was placing a sheet over Mister John's entire body. "Is he...d e a d...Suh?" "Indeed Bob, passed peacefully in his sleep about an hour ago. If only our other patients could pass as peacefully as he did. He apparently really enjoyed visiting with y'all, and greatly appreciated your coming. We simply don't have any medicine to fight infections in our hospitals right now. If an arm or a leg gets infected we have to cut if off at the source, and if it spreads after that there's nothing we can do. It breaks our hearts as a staff to not be able to provide the best care possible. Gentlemen, we're very sorry for your loss. George, whenever you're ready I'll have some nurses come get his body, and place it in a coffin for the long journey home, and load it onto the wagon. I'll let y'all spend a little bit more time with him, and then when you're ready, George, come meet me in my office. Thank you."

There was silence in the room for a long time, and then Bob couldn't help it, and he started crying. He wished he could stop, but the flood of tears kept right on coming until he was completely dry inside. One of the nurses helped him to a chair and comforted him. The nurse was Mizz Ophelia Johnson. Mister Joe just stared at the corpse that the night before had been his brother, and then he knew his brother was no longer in that body, but was in his spiritual body as the preacher liked to say when you pass away.

Mister Joe was 25 years old, and now both of his older brothers had been killed by the Yankees.

What a cost this war was having on his family. Pop would be devastated, as Bob had pointed out. For John Thomas was his oldest, & probably his favorite, though when asked by anyone he would always say, "Suh, I love all my boys the same, equally." Susan, his wife, will be devastated, they were married 17 years, and the last 3 of 'em the Yankees had stolen from her, and her a widow now at such a young age.

Finally Mister Joe spoke, "Ashes to ashes. Dust to dust. The Lord giveth, and the Lord taketh away. Blessed be the name of the Lord." With that he walked out of the room, slowly followed by Mister Bob, then myself. Mister Bob gave me a hug, then thanked me for taking him back home like I did for Mister James. Mister Joe stuck out his hand, and I shook it. "George, thank you ever so much for all your help. We look forward to being home with you soon, and start living, and stop having to worry about all this dying." "Yes suh, I look forward to those days ahead." "Thank you again, George, you take care, and tell the family we said hello, and thank you for your prayers," said Mister Joe, then they were out of sight. I went back into the room and told Mizz Johnson that we truly appreciated all the care she gave to Mister John, and so did he. "I surely wish we could've done more, George." "No ma'am, I believe y'all did all y'all could for him and then some." "Thank you George, you're too kind. Have a safe trip back home to Georgia, and I'll say a prayer y'all make it back safe and sound." With that, I bowed out of there and went to find Colonel

Wilkerson. He was in his office, so I knocked before I went in. When he looked up over his spectacles, he saw me and said, "George, George. Come in, come in. Have a seat, George. I'm so sorry for your loss. Are you ready for me to have the orderlies load Major Carson onto your wagon?" "Yes suh, I'm ready." "Good. I'll have 'em take care of everything. You can just wait here 'til I get back. I'll be right back."

He was back in 30 minutes, and said, "Okay George, you're all set.

Thank you for your devotion to Major Carson. Have a safe trip home George, I wish I was going with you." "Thank you, suh. You will be soon I'm sure." Then before I knew it we were out of there. Mister John and me, 'cept it was just his casket now. "Oh Lawd, God of heaven, and God of earth. Please get thy servants Mister John Thomas Carson and myself safely back home to Georgia. May his life be a legacy unto thy great glory and love. Comfort his bereaved family Lawd Jesus, and grant them thy Shalom. In Jesus' name I pray Father, Amen."

So, we were off. Friday September 30th, 1864, a little over three years since we first got here by train. Lawd, I was anxious to be home with Lula but not like this. At 10 a.m. we were leaving the hospital in Lynchburg, VA for the last time ever I hoped for that place was also the final resting place for Mister James two years ago.

We made good travel on our first day going back home and by 10 P.M. we'd made it to Mount Airy, N.C. The folks there were nice enough I reckon, and when a farmer learned I was carrying a dead Confederate soldier home for final burial he opened up his home to me, which was very kind since it was late and all. In the morning after a big breakfast, Farmer Joe bid us adieu, whatever that meant.

On Saturday we didn't fare as well as we did the day before because of a vicious thunderstorm all day, likes of which I ain't seen in a while. I put on my straw hat, didn't help much though. Wish we had one of them covered wagons like you see in Harpers Weekly to keep the rain out. I found a copy of the magazine at a little shop today on my way home. Seems like all they were interested in talking about was politics. Somebody named McClellan and another gentleman named Pendleton nobody ever heard of.

Chapter 16

The horse Colonel Wilkerson had was a beautiful mare, so I named her Sheba, like the Queen whom King Solomon bedazzled. We got along just fine and a little after dark we pulled into a town called Gastonia, North Carolina. Another kind farmer put us up for the night, and after a quick breakfast we were on the road by 7:00 o'clock in the morning. Hopefully we'd be at Crazy Charley's house in Lavonia by nightfall. I felt bad about travelling on the Sabbath, but I figured the good Lawd would allow it since I had to get Mister John's body home as fast as I could so they could bury him.

About an hour after we crossed back into the great state of Georgia we pulled up in front of Crazy Charley's house. "Charley, you inside?" After a minute I heard his familiar voice, "George, that you?" "Yeah it's me. Good to see you again. Mind putting up with me again for one more night?" "Naw, George, don't mind atall. Glad to have company. What you got in the back of your wagon?" "That's Mister John Thomas Carson. The Yankees finally killed him as a result of injuries sustained from the 3rd Battle of Winchester." "Good Lawd, George! That's his oldest boy right?" "Sure is. The other two are still in Virginia fighting Yankees." "How'd they get him, George, if you don't mind me asking?" "He was wounded three times in the battle. The third time they shot him in the stomach. Anyhow, he was in the hospital in Lynchburg, VA for 11 days, and they had to cut off his leg. Problem is the Yankees have blockaded all medicine from coming into the South. Thus, we have to pray our injured and wounded men don't get infected. 'Cause if they do, they're gonna die. It's that simple Charley." "My word, I'm real sorry for your loss George. You wanna get that pretty horse of yer's fed and watered, then come on up to the house & we'll eat? You know you ain't gotta knock, just come on in." "Thanks, Charley."

"Thanks for putting us up for the night again, Charley, and it's so good to see ya again." "Pleasure's all mine, George. Good to have some company again for a change." "I reckon it's been over two years since I saw you last, what you been up to?" "Well, let's see. You was last here two years ago right?" "Yep, two years ago. That's right." "O.k., not much. Things have been pretty much the same round here. Oh, I did get married after you was last here." "You did? Congratulations! Where is she?" "I reckon I met her at prayer meeting one Sunday night. Her name is Daisy Mae Flanders. Didn't take my name after we was married. Said she was from Duck Town, "where's that," say's I, and she said in Forsyth County. To which I replied, "Same question," and she said, "It's about 85 miles over yonder," as she pointed back west over her shoulder.

Anyhow, we got married the next day love at first sight I reckon then two weeks after we got married said she was leaving me for a Yankee soldier she met at the market. At first I was heartbroken George, then after that I just said, 'all right, that's the way you feel, the go on, git on outta heah woman before I thrash you with my cane,' and she was gone. Never seen her since." Charley didn't say anything for a while, so finally I said, "Real sorry to hear that Charley. Don't sound like it was meant to be." "Naw, I reckon you're right there George. Maybe I'll find true love one day again. George, why do women gotta be so complicated? It just tears me up sometimes that here I am, 72 years old, and in all that time I ain't never been able to find the right woman for me. Why you reckon that is, George?" "Charley if I had to guess, I'd say that's 'cause you ain't met her yet. When you meet her you'll know."

Charley and I had a good visit that night, and in the morning I was glad to get on the road with an early start. By 6:30 in the morning, Mister John, Sheba, and myself were on the road to Reynolds. It was Monday, and as we were getting closer to a home that we hadn't seen in years I was pretty happy. It was a month and one day since the City of Atlanta had fallen to the Yankees. Rumor had it the Yankees were gonna march to the Sea at Savannah, and take and burn anything that ain't nailed down. Hope I can get back home before they make it out to our home so I can help Lula, and Mister Carson hide our livestock in the swamp so the Yankees can't steal 'em. Around high noon I made my way through Athens, and saw a lot of boys from the college there building revetments all around the college. One of 'em told me they were putting this up in case the Yankees came through Athens. Knowing a bunch of poorly armed college boys didn't stand a chance against the Yankee Army machine I bid him good day, and took my leave. The roads were eerily quiet on the way to Reynolds.

Almost as if folks were scared to come outside and be seen by the Yankees or something. I hadn't seen any myself yet which was good. At least the weather was agreeable, unlike the other day when everything I had on was soaked to the bone. It was neither too hot nor too cold but just right with no wind.

My boots had finally dried out from that monsoon we rode through in South Carolina the other day. Lawd have mercy! I wonder if it was a hurricane? Sure did seem bad enough to be one, that's for sure!!!

What's Mister Carson gonna think when he sees me pull up with Mister John in his Pine Box? I shudder to think, but I'm sure he'll be devastated. "Lawd Jesus, please keep Joe and Bob safe and sound up there in Ole Virginny. Be with Mizz Susan over the loss of her beloved husband Mister John. Thank you for keeping me safe for the last 3 years Father God. Help us to make the remainder of the journey home safely Father. In Jesus' great name I pray, Amen."

Ah, look at all that Red Georgia Clay! Lula can't stand it 'cause *"it be getting everywhere, and you can't hardly clean it all up."* I secretly loved it, though I won't be sharing that with her anytime soon. Look at all them Pine trees. Pine trees and Georgia clay, Lawd have mercy, it's great to be home finally! At 7:00 o'clock that night I made it to the town of Locust Grove, GA. As I rode through the town I made my way on to the Jones plantation. Mister Jones is a friend of Mister Carson, and he should be able to put me up for the night. As I turned off the highway onto his drive, first thing I noticed were empty fields that used to grow cotton as far as the eye could see. The Live Oaks were still there lining the driveway, pretty as ever. "Well, George Carson, how ya doing young man?" "Mighty fine Mister Jones, mighty fine suh! I hope & pray things are well with y'all?" "About as well as they can be. We hear that Scamp Sherman is about to come through here on his way to the Sea, and try to burn down every plantation on the way, while taking all the food & livestock to boot. We all heard what you did for James years back, right nice of you George!" It was at that point that he saw the coffin in the back, and said, "Who's in the coffin, George?" "Suh, that's Mister John Thomas, he was wounded at the 3rd Battle of Winchester, then spent 11 days in the hospital at Lynchburg, VA before he succumbed to infection and passed away peacefully in his sleep. Bless his heart."

Mister Jones was solemn for a moment then he told me that 3 of his 6 sons had died in this "blasted war," and he was ready for it to be over with so they could go back to the way things used to be.

"J.J.'s gonna be devastated I say. Poor Susan, she's gonna be most heartbroken. George, if you'll hand the reins to big Jim here, he'll take care of your mare, and you can come inside and tell me all about this miserable war, and we'll find you something to eat." "Thank you, suh. Here you go Jim."

After a meal fit for a king, Mister Jones and I retired to his front porch and sat in his rockers enjoying the beautiful sunset. "George, do you really feel this war is over? That General Lee is fighting as long as he can for the sole purpose of saving his dignity?" "Yes suh, that sounds about right. In every battle I witnessed, suh, and I watched a heap of 'em, the Yankees always outnumbered us 2 to 1. Sometimes it seemed like it was 3 to 1, but that didn't matter to our boys. They fought with a dignity and a zeal the Yankees don't have. If the Yankees did have that zeal, this war would've been over two years ago. Suh, as far as I can tell it'll all be over by next summer, and then we'll have to deal with the fallout of the war, and the reparations the Yankees will certainly make us pay. I reckon it ain't gonna be pretty after the war for a while suh, but, with the good Lawd's help 'this too shall pass.'" Mister Jones puffed on his corn cob pipe he got from a friend in Missouri a good bit before he said anything. "You're right, George, 'this too shall pass,' hopefully before the Yankees destroy us all. Good night, George, it was real nice talking to ya, and we can talk more at breakfast before you head off back home to Reynolds." "Yes suh, it was great talking to you as well. Many thanks for your splendid hospitality." "Glad to do it George, good night." "Good night suh." There was a sliver of moon out, and the cicada's were a buzzing, it was great to almost be home!

At first they would be sad to see me 'cause of Mister John and all, but soon after that I'm sure we can all have a happy reunion.

Hopefully, Lula will have my favorite meal for me when I get home: Country fried steak, mashed potatoes and gravy, corn on the cob, corn bread, and if I'm lucky she might even make red velvet cake. If'n she don't make a red velvet cake, that's okay too 'cause it'll be great to finally be home after three years!

Stop worrying about food I told myself and worry about getting Mister John home safe and sound after this long journey. "Lawd have mercy on Mister Joe and Mister Bob, 'cause surely Lawd you'll let at least one or two of Mister Carson's sons survive this awful war. Thank you, Lawd, in Jesus' great name I pray, Amen." I smoked my pipe on his front porch a little while longer, staring up at the beautiful sky. There was no moon out tonight, but heaven's sake, those stars sure were pretty.

In the morning, I begged my leave as soon as I could, and I was off. Sheba even looked happy to be home in Georgia as well. Not long after I started off I passed through Griffin, and Camp Stephens. They had a lot of railroad lines going through the city, going from there up to Atlanta. Somebody told me once that they printed a lot of Confederate money in Griffin, and a fella even told me they even printed *their own currency*. I still had a lot of that Confederate money, but reckoned it wasn't worth the paper it was printed on. Up in Virginia it wasn't unheard of for women to take wheel barrows of it to market to purchase a loaf of bread. Lawd have mercy!

As the sun was almost all the way up in the sky we passed through Barnesville. Folks were real polite, and we exchanged smiles and waves. Not much farther, not much farther, Sheba, and then all our troubles will be over. Would all of our troubles be over? Probably not, but leastways we'd be home again.

Mister John had written some letters he wanted me to give to the family. As we were getting closer and closer to Reynolds, I could not for the life of me get the words of Mister John's letter to his son Albert out of my head, try though as I may.

Dear Albert,

Son, the Surgeon had to amputate my leg, and they're hoping it won't get infected. Should that be the case, they don't have any medicine to fight it….and I won't have much time left. You however are almost a man now, and should anything happen to me you <u>must</u> take good care of your mother, son. She is a genteel lady, and you must always honor her by being a gentleman in & out of her presence. We own a large farm son, and being that you've always been smart, I'm sure you'll know how to run it when we have to free the servants. Most of them will stay I'm sure. Should you ever need any gentlemanly advice you may ask George anything. The good Lord has endowed him with a wealth

*of knowledge about many topics, and he's
always good company. Thank the good Lord
for him!!! One thing I'm proud of son is
that this horrible war should be over well
before you turn 18. The next 5 to 10 years
after it should be hard on everybody in the
South, but I trust that with hard work &
perseverance, "this too shall pass." You've
been in my thoughts and prayers for over
three years. Make me proud, and please take
great care of your mother. To do so would
mean that my sacrifice wouldn't have been
in vain.*

Your loving father,
Pop

Mister John, Sheba, and myself were getting closer
and closer to Reynolds, I was feeling kind of giddy, like
a school boy on Christmas morn. I reckon an old man
can sometimes get excited the same as a young man
can. But that giddiness quickly turned to sadness as the
three of us passed by Mister John's large plantation on
the north side of Taylor County. When he bought the

property right before the war he had gotten a great deal on a lot of land, and he loved working that land with all his soul. For three years all Mister John seemed to be able to talk about every night around the camp fire was how he couldn't wait to get back to his plantation and walk through the fields, and smell the rarified Georgia air, on his own land, and not have to worry about getting killed by the Yankees.

And now here he was being driven by his old plantation in a pine box, instead of sitting up in the carriage with me. Such a shame! Such injustice to such a wonderful gentleman. Mister John Thomas, you suh shall surely be missed suh. Indeed suh, for a finer gentleman I have never known.

As we drove past Mister John's driveway, here came Mizz Susan and Mister Albert in their horse and buggy on their way to town. We saw each other at the same time, and she yelled out "GEORGE! Is that him, is that my dear husband in the back of your wagon?" "Fraid so ma'am. I'm so sorry for y'all!" Albert pulled their buggy next to mine and helped his gentle mother out of the wagon. She ran over to mine, and quite nearly tripped, and burst into such a flood of tears as I have never seen before!

Mister Albert's eyes started to tear up, but then he wiped 'em off with his handkerchief and said, "George, thank you ever so much for all that you've done for Father during the war. He loved you like a second Pop! Always talked about you in his letters about how despite the miserable conditions, you always found a way to lessen 'em. For that, from the bottom of my heart suh, thank you." Then he shook my hand again firmly, but not too hard like some young bucks like to. Silently, we walked over to where Mizz Susan was. She being through weeping was trying to recover her bearings again. Then she walked over to me and gave me a hug, then a kiss on the cheek. "George, I know I can never repay you for your kindness to my dear husband suh, please just know that if there's ever anything you or Lula need, if we have it, it's yours. Now may we head out to Mister Carson's house so we can get him in the ground tomorrow with a proper Christian burial." "Yes ma'am," I tipped my hat to her & said, "happy to be of service to y'all."

Mister Albert helped his mother back into the wagon and caught her when she almost fell out. Must've almost fainted or something, anyhow, that young man caught her with a gentle grace, built on strength the likes of which I hadn't seen in I don't know how long, but it reminded me of something I couldn't figure out. Later on that week it hit me.

He reminded me of Mister John at that age, a quiet gentleman, with grace, and the strength of an ox. Almost as if Mister John was speaking to me from the grave maybe. About 3:00 o'clock in the afternoon both of our wagons passed through Reynolds, and folks on the streets were quiet, ladies in extra wide hoop skirts dabbed at their eyes as they saw Mister John's casket. Gentlemen stood ramrod straight at attention. They all took off their hats and covered their hearts with it. How they loved him! Mister John had friends all over the county, all spoke highly of him. I never heard a cross word spoken about him behind his back. Well, we'd covered over 500 miles this trip and had only 5 miles left to travel. "Think you got 5 more miles left in your legs Sheba?" She snorted, as if to say *"I've got another 5,000 miles left in me!"* We turned off the highway onto River Road. Thank goodness it's October, even though the gnats can be a nuisance sometimes 'til December, they're out of control in the summertime. As we pulled into the drive up to the house, Mister Carson was on the porch smoking his pipe. I waved at him, he waved back. A simple greeting between two old friends, then the front door opened, next thing I heard was, *"George! George 'DAT YOU HONEY, OR YOU HIS GHOST?"* "It ain't my ghost baby, it's me! Come see for yourself!" She ran over and hugged me, almost knocking me down.

"Thank de Lawd, Honey, you back, 'cause he answered my prayers! Every night I say, 'oh Lawd please bring George back soon's you can. Thank ya Lawd, Amen. All right, OUTTA MY WAY! Honey, I'm gone make yo favorite meal for supper, country fried steak." With that she stormed into the house, nearly knocking over anyone or anything unfortunate enough to be in the way.

I went up on the porch to Mister Carson who stood up and shook my hand. Softly he said, "George, from the bottom of my heart, thank you for bringing back my boy. Don't beat yourself over the head for his untimely demise. I hear there was nothing the surgeon nor the nurses could do for him without any medicines to treat him with, other than licker for the pain. Have a seat, my friend." He didn't say much for a while, so I lit my pipe and relaxed.

Riding all the way from Ole Virginny in a wagon can give you lumbago something fierce and praise the Lawd it hadn't got to me on this last journey! We sat in glorious silence for a while, looking out over the empty fields that used to be full of cotton as far as the eye could see. They had been replaced with vegetables in some sections but not all. Then we talked about the war, and what he thought about it, what I thought about it, and what everybody else thought of it. "Suh, before I forget, Mister John asked me to give you this." I handed him the envelope, as he took it he said, "What is it, George?" "Reckon it's a letter, suh." He took his time opening it, then put on his reading spectacles.

Dear Pop,

If you're reading this it means that I have passed, & George is back with you at home. Suh, the Yankees were really handing it to us at 3rd Battle of Winchester, & we had to retreat. During that time I received my 3rd mortal wound. The irony is that if the Yankees hadn't blockaded the South, they could've treated my wounds easily, & I'd be back fighting with my men. Often outgunned, almost always having to battle a Yankee Army double our size, it is my honor suh to let you know we gave them no mercy, with all we had these past 3 years. I suspect the war will be over within a year, probably sooner. Even though the Yankees will more than likely win the war, they will NEVER break the spirit of a Southern man, & for that I am honored to have served with some of the most noble, humble, strong, & patriotic men you ever saw. I've instructed young Albert to take charge of my estate. I reckon no matter the outcome of the war, or the price we'll have to pay for it, young Albert will be more than a capable manager of my estate. Also, I've instructed him to rely on George for guidance should he need any. I am saddened to not see you again in this life, but am eager to in the next.

Your loving son,
John Thomas

He took out his handkerchief and dabbed at his eyes. Carefully folded it, and stuck it back in his coat pocket. "George, am I gonna have *any sons left* when the last battle is fought in this horrible war?" "Yes suh, you should. Mister Joe is leader of the Sharpshooters, so they're always a long ways from the fighting men up front, and Mister Robert is courier for the Generals, so he's never in too much danger, so hopefully your two youngest will come home with no problems." He considered this for a moment. "Yes, I suppose you're right. It just concerns me greatly that the Yankees might get my last two sons, and then I'll have nobody left." "Yes suh, that's understandable. Reckon we gotta keep praying to the good Lawd, and hope he answers our prayers." "Indeed. I ain't much concerned about Joseph. He's got a good head on his shoulders. I'm concerned about Robert, and how he wants to be a front line trooper so bad it's killing him. I hope he doesn't do anything stupid like volunteering for a dangerous mission, or anything like that. 'Cause I know he'll leap at the chance to something crazy like that and so do you unfortunately." "Yes suh, that's a good point, and I can see him doing that as well. Mister John was able to get General Gordon to arrange for him to be a courier for Generals Dole and Cook. Luckily he was in a spot to be able to do that. Otherwise I reckon he'd be a frontline trooper like everybody else." "Thank heaven for that, George! Thank heaven!"

Supper that night was phenomenal! Just when I was about to tell Lula how good it was and how Mister Sam could almost cook as good, I quickly shut my mouth. In fact, I had to place my hand over my mouth to keep it from my undoing on the day I got home. Seeing this, she said, "George what de matter with you Honey you look like you bout to pitch a fit or something baby." "Naw dear, I thought a gnat was trying to fly into my mouth, so I was trying to keep it out." "Mmmmm hmmmmmmm, looked to me like you bout say something, then yo head got de better of yo mouth. What you gone say? I won't yell at ya, honey." I leaned back in my chair to have a better chance to duck if frying pans were to become flying missiles being flung at me.

"Well....Honey, at the hospital in Lynchburg, Virginia they had this cook in the mess hall named Mister Sam, and, um..." "um nothing, everybody heard bout dat cook named Mista Sam Honey. They all go on bout how gooda cook he be, & dis & dat I hear from all de injured soldiers home on furlough." "So you heard about his cooking Honey?" "*Everybody* heard bout it Baby. And I's glad y'all got to eat good up in dat hospital up dere, Honey. Now if'n he wanted to come down heah to Jawja, reckon we could have a contest to see who de best 'tween us." I let my breath out, and took a huge breath. Guess I was holding it in anticipation of a storm. It sure was great to be back in my home, and to be near my lovely wife! "Honey, I've got to go see Mizz Susan real quick, then I'll be right back." "What you gotta see her fo?" "Gotta give her a letter from Mister John." "Oh dear Lawd have mercy! Dat gone tear dat po thang up."

It took about an hour at an easy pace for Sheba to get us to their house. Mister Albert opened the door, and I shook his hand, and asked to see his mother, Mizz Susan. I waited in the parlor while he went & got her. She came into the parlor while I had my back turned looking at some of Mister John's books. "He spent a lot of time in here. Usually he was reading, or writing letters, or some such thing. Often he received guests in this room." I about jumped outta my skin! It ain't good to sneak up on an old man like that. After I felt my heart wasn't gonna explode, I quickly turned around & said real gently, "I don't wanna waste any of your time Mizz Susan. Mister John wanted me to give this letter to you when we got back. I'll show myself out, ma'am. Good night." As I handed it to her, I heard her say, "Good night George." Mizz Susan

took a seat in Mister John's favorite chair & opened
the letter.

My dearest wife Susan,

*I have thought about you every day, &
especially every night for over 3 years now.
Unfortunately, I was wounded three times
at the 3rd Battle of Winchester. If we weren't
blockaded by the Yankees up and down the
east coast, there would be medicine to heal
me, but, because of the blockade there isn't
any at all.*

*I told Albert via a letter, similar to the
one to you, that he was now in charge of my
estate and to look after you and treat you
gently. I have full faith & confidence that
he will execute his duties with due diligence
in these matters. Furthermore, y'all will
also have George to lend you a hand should
need be.*

*Should I never see you again in this life
my dear, know that having you there by my
side in marriage these last 17 years has made*

me the happiest man in the world. To see
you again in the next life gives me strength to
make it through the pain of this one.

Your loving husband,
John T.

Mizz Susan stared frozen like at the letter for a full 5 minutes before she did anything else. A few tears started to fall from her eyes, nothing like this afternoon though. "What a fine gentleman my husband was." Between sniffles she said, "thank you Lord Jesus for the memory of my husband John. May his life not have been lived in vain, but use his fidelity to you, & to his nation to leave a legacy for someone else to claim one day. Thank you so much Lord for giving him to me for 17 years! In Jesus' great name I pray, Amen."

The next morning, on Friday October 7th, 1864 we buried Mister John in the cemetery right next to his brother James. Reverend Glover gave an eloquent eulogy, which comforted the family greatly. After a brief grave side service, the family had a host of guests and visitors to mourn with.

The funeral service was at 9:00 a.m., and by 10:00 the house was bustling with activity. Lula got up extra early to cook for all the guests and visitors. This day she outdid even herself. Must've been 50 people in the house, and all of 'em went home stuffed, but here's the thing, *here's the thing of it*, she cooked it all herself. Rest of the servants knew better than to try and go in the kitchen when she was in it.

Chapter 17

At the funeral, Mizz Susan was dressed in all black, from head to toe. She did real well at the funeral too. Reckon she had cried herself out yesterday.

I found Mister Carson on the porch, all alone smoking his pipe. "George, come join me, my friend!" "Yes suh, be happy to." "I thought it was a lovely funeral, George, not too long, nor too short. What'd you think, George?" "Yes suh, I agree. It was just right." We sat there smoking our pipes in blessed silence.

When you get to be as old as we are, you learn how to sit back and relax in blessed silence. With our ages combined, they are well over 120 years, so I reckon we've seen a thing or two in our days here on earth.

"George, I hope the war will be over before I have to go to any more funerals for my boys. This is getting ridiculous. I'm not worried about Joseph, but Robert frightens me with his risky attitude."

"Suh, you want me to go back up there and look after 'em two youngins of yours? I'd be happy to do it." "No George, I believe they'll be fine on their own up there in Virginia. You take care of your dear wife Lula, for she has been such a mighty comfort to me these past 3 years. Lord have mercy, if I hadn't had her, I reckon I'd had a nervous breakdown. Thanks for offering though, George. Hopefully this war will be over soon, and we'll all be a family once again soon my friend."

Throughout the rest of the day folks came and went throughout the house to offer their condolences to Mizz Susan, and Mister Carson. The rest of the fall of '64 came and went with a blur, as well as the wintertime of 1865. Home we were all hoping for a quick end of the war so things could get back to normal. Well, it was quiet except Sherman coming through in the fall of '64. When he arrived in Reynolds we had already hidden almost all of the livestock in the swamp. However, they did manage to steal Mister Carson's favorite horse. He was mighty steamed about that, but quickly moved on to other things. I will say this about them Yankees though, one of 'em gave one of my grandchildren his very first piece of candy!

We got word at the end of March of Joe's daring attack and subsequent capture of Fort Stedman, VA from the Yankees on Saturday, March 25th, 1865. With his daring band of Sharpshooters, and their amazing Whitworth rifles, Mister Joe's men captured Fort Stedman in the middle of the night.

With a force of just a few hundred under his command, Captain Joe P. Carson captured several thousand Yankees that night, but it was all for naught, as the Yankees were just a few short days away from complete victory against the Army of Northern Virginia. Mister Carson wouldn't have two sons survive this horrible war. Just one, for after his successful capture of the Fort, Mister Joseph began to look for Mister Robert, and one of the men under his command told him where he'd last seen him, and believed him to be dead. Sure enough, Mister Joe found him right where the other soldier said he thought he'd last seen him. He recognized the coat he had let his brother borrow the night before. He beckoned the other soldier to help him carry Mister Robert's lifeless body out of the fight. As they were carrying him out of the battle, they were being shot at by some Yankees who obviously had no respect for the dead. Mister Robert's body sustained many more bullet wounds while they carried him off the battlefield. Mister

Joseph buried him near the battleground in a spot where he was sure to remember where he buried young Robert's poor body. Mister Robert passed away from this world on Saturday, March 25th, 1865, and with his passing Mister Carson had now lost his two oldest sons, as well as his youngest one. Lawd have mercy! Luckily though, Mister Joe would indeed survive the war, and be around for years to tell war stories to anyone who asked him for one. After church the next day, the telegraph officer dispatched a man to come out to Mister Carson's house to tell him Robert had passed on from this life.

Sunday March 26, 1865

Dear Pop,

It's with great regret & solitude I must inform you that Robert is dead. He was shot & killed during our successful capture of Ft. Stedman. I buried him next to the battlefield in a location I shant forget. I am quite sorry suh to have to write this news to you.

Your loving son,
Joseph

Chapter 18

We were on Mister Carson's front porch after church when he got the news. A negro man came riding up the drive in a huff, likes of which I hadn't seen in a while. Mister Carson probably knew the telegram concerned either Mister Joe or Mister Bob, so I reckon it wasn't too much of a shock for him to read the telegram. He handed it to me when he was through reading it and thanked the man for coming out to the house and bringing it to him.

For a while neither of us said anything, we were too shocked by the way death had come unto Carson House in the last 3 years of this war and wondered if any of his sons would make it out of it alive. It was a while before Mister Carson spoke, then he let out a loud breath, blew some smoke from his pipe, then he pointed his pipe at me. "My dear, George, would you kindly go get my son Robert and bring him home, suh?" "Yes suh, I'd be happy too." Next morning I loaded up Colonel Wilkerson's wagon, and hitched the Queen of Sheba to it. We were off to Virginia again. Lula wasn't happy about me having to go back and all, but, she was glad it was just gonna be a short trip. Mister Carson gave me plenty of money, Confederate and Shinplasters to get me there and back. He even gave me a little gold in case I needed to bribe my way out of any trouble with the Yankees. It was Saturday, April 1st when I arrived near Mister Robert's graveside. Mister Joe showed me where he'd buried his brother, and then we both dug him up. Mister Carson had placed an empty coffin in my wagon, which I had taken with me all the way from Georgia. As we gently placed his body in the coffin, Mister Joe nailed it shut, thus ending a life way too young, and so far away from his native Georgia. Mister Robert never had a chance to get married and raise a family, and the poor thing died a week before he turned 19. Lawd have mercy! Way too young to pass away! Wanting to get back home to Lula for good this time, I told Mister Joseph to take care of his self, and the war'd probably be over in the next few days anyway. "Try and survive this war, Mister Joe, 'cause I'm tired of having to bring your dead brothers back to Reynolds, and your father." "Will do, George, will do! Thank you for all you do for Pop and our family. I'll be home soon. Have a safe trip home." "Yes suh, thank you again for your help with Mister Robert's body, and *you take care of yours suh!*"

Having made this trip so many times now with Mister Carson's deceased boys was becoming a habit for me now. *"Dear Lawd in heaven please let this be the last time I have to do this. Please Lawd Jesus keep Mister Joseph safe for the rest of the war father. In Jesus' great name I pray, Amen."*

I hustled to get Mister Robert's body back as fast as I could, so they could give him a proper Christian burial and all. Then a week later I was home. As I pulled up into the driveway for the third time with one of Mister Carson's deceased sons, I felt empty inside. Sorta dead myself, I reckon a little bit of me died each time I transported his dead sons back to the great state of Georgia from Virginia.

They had the funeral the next day for Mister Robert at the Carson family cemetery. The little plot is about a stone throw from the house. If you're facing Mister Carson's house, the cemetery is slightly forward of his house, and towards the left. It seemed like half of

Reynolds, and *all* of Macon County chose to attend Mister Robert's funeral. He was well liked, and half the single ladies of the County were hoping to snare him unto marriage when he came home from the War Between the States. The preacher gave a fine eulogy for Mister Robert. Don't remember a better one than the one the preacher gave that day, & not a dry eye was to be found. Mister Carson tried his best to keep his bearing, but even he could not contain a few small tears for his youngest son. While everyone else was listening to the preacher, Mister Carson was scolding himself for letting him get out of his courier job, and go on that raid with Joseph's Sharpshooters! For young Robert had actually written his father to ask his permission to go on raids with Joseph, and he had given him his blessing. For he knew Mister Robert would never go behind his back if he couldn't get his father's blessing. He so wanted to honor his father in all he did. Perhaps this was also because his real mother had died when he was only 16, and he couldn't stand to be in the presence of his stepmother, the former Mizz Mary Laura Lamar Slappey. So whenever he could, he sought out his father after his mother had passed, and while at an age when most teenage boys want to rebel against their fathers, because they don't think their daddies are very smart, Mister Robert was different than 'em. He *wanted* his father's blessings. He wanted toappare please him, and not to cause him worry like other fellas his age were wont to do. Mister Carson thought to himself, "if I'd told him no, do your courier job instead, he'd probably be alive. And now he's dead, and it might as well have been me who pulled the trigger on him."

Then just as that thought occurred to him, the preacher told the assembled audience, "Robert was a courier for Generals Dole and Cook. About a month ago he wrote his father asking for permission to go on raids with his brother Joseph. His father knowing full well that he would never go behind his back if he didn't give him his blessing, with great trepidation, and after a long night of prayer, Mister Carson made the decision to allow him his blessing to go on the raids with Captain Joseph." At this point at the graveside service there was not a dry eye in the audience. The preacher looked Mister Carson right in the eye, then he said, "Suh, don't second guess your decision. You asked the good Lord for wisdom, and guidance on how to answer his question. When you gave him your blessing you were walking in faith that he would take care of your son Robert. Just know suh, he's now with our dear Lord in heaven, in glory. A place we all esteem to be at one day, & young Robert is there now preparing a place for us as we speak." At this point, all the young women could not control themselves any longer & were crying out hysterically, *"Robert! Robert! We were gonna be wed when you came back from the war!"* If the women weren't so distraught at young Robert's early demise, they would have realized that about 5 or 6 of 'em just said the exact same thing. At this point, Lula and I made eye contact and winked at each other. Mister Robert had always been a ladies man, but apparently much more so than even I knew. Oh, you'll be missed Mister Robert. You'll surely be missed my friend.

A few months later, the recently released confederate soldiers began to slowly make their way home. Mister Carson's only son to survive the war, Joseph made it home, along with all the others fortunate enough to survive the awful war, and came back home to houses that weren't there anymore, and communities decimated by the ravages of war.

Since Lincoln had freed all the slaves, when the war was finally over Mister Carson called all his servants together, and he stood on the front porch, and addressed all of us.

"Good morning y'all, by now you've probably heard that President Lincoln freed all the slaves in the South recently, and I'm happy to tell you all this. Each and every one of you is now a free man, and a free woman." Some of the younger servants cried out with a joy you ain't never seen before. Then he continued, "That being said. From this moment forward, if you don't want to work for me anymore, I appreciate your many faithful years of service to my family, and y'all are free to leave. Now, I'd like to have all of you stay and I'll be happy to pay y'all, or work out some type of arrangement that is mutually beneficial for the both of us. That's all I have for you folks. Thank you for attention." Some of the younger servants, men and women, were outta there in 15 minutes. But, for the most part, most of his servants decided to stick around, and make a go of it. Where were they gonna go? They had nowhere to go, for this was where their family and friends were. Lula and I had decided years ago that this is our home and should this opportunity arise, we would choose to stay on our house and on our land. When General Sherman's Yankees made their famous run through Georgia, Mister Carson's property was mostly spared, 'cept they did take his favorite horse when they came through our area.

The smart farmers hid their livestock in the swamp by the river so the Yankees couldn't take any of 'em, & it wasn't unheard of for ladies to wear every single dress they owned when the Yankees came riding through, sometimes 5 or 6 of 'em worn right on top of the other.

When Mister Carson's younger servants eager to depart, started walking up River Road on the way towards Macon, Atlanta, and even up North, they all to a man had that glint in their eyes that said, "We're going to enjoy our freedom and go live in the cities as free men." What they soon discovered shocked 'em when they reached their new destinations up North, to learn that they weren't wanted there. Though the Yankees may have won the war, a soft prejudice still existed, and most of the newly freed slaves realized they actually had it pretty good working for Mister Carson. Most of 'em had their own houses of some form or another. And even when the Yankees nearly succeeded in starving the South to death, the folks at Mister Carson's house generally ate better than the rest.

'Course there were some lean years during the war, but they generally made it through the lean years because of proper planning on Lula's behalf. For if there was one thing she was really good at, it was seeing that the shelves in her pantry and in the barn would always remain at the correct levels.

It was real relaxing to sit on Mister Carson's porch with him in the afternoons, and we'd smoke our pipes, thanking the good Lawd the awful war was over. Though things were a little different now, we were all willing to make a go at life in the New South. One afternoon about a year after the war ended, Mister Carson, Joe, and myself were sitting on the front porch smoking our pipes. Not a care in the world, enjoying the sunset, with the cicada's performing their usual orchestra at night for us. Next thing we knew, here came Big Sam walking down the road with his wife Sue Ellen. When they got to the porch, they stayed in the grass, and Big Sam tipped his straw hat at us, and said, "Good evening Mista Carson, gentlemen." "Hey Sam! How'd it go for y'all up in Ohio?" "Well suh, I reckon it ain't as nice for blacks up theah as it be heah in Jawja. Dem folks talk 'bout freeing blacks men and all, but I reckon dey don't see us as free as 'dey is. They still 'spect us to do de jobs dey won't do, so last week I told myself, 'self, we outta heah.' We going back home to Mista Carson house ifun he take me back. So I tolt Sue Ellen to pack our suitcases 'cause we coming home. And heah we be suh, ifun we can have our old jobs back?" "Why 'course y'all can have your old jobs back, Sam! I'd be delighted to have y'all back here with us. Y'all are part of our family, your old cottage is empty, and I believe I can hear it calling your names." With that, Mister Carson stood up & walked over to 'em and gave both a handshake and a friendly hug. "Oh, & y'all must be starving, so go inside & have Lula fix y'all up something to eat." "Thank you suh, from de bottom of my heart. Thank you!" "My pleasure, Sam."

Epilogue

It was about 9 years later that Mister Carson passed away as well. It was on a Thursday morning, October 21, 1875. He passed quietly in his sleep sometime during the night. The next day we had the funeral, and a lot of folks came and said real nice things about him, for he was the finest gentleman I've ever known.

About 12 years after that the good Lawd took my Lula from me, back unto his glory. She got the flu something fierce, and then when I was holding her while she was in bed, she said, "George, Baby do you know how much I love you?" With that special smile in her eyes, I asked her the same, and then she closed her eyes for the last time.

It's now a couple of years later, and I'm really getting up there in age now. Have to use a cane when I walk. One night as Mister Joseph and I were sitting on the front porch enjoying the view, he asked me, "George, you remember the first time we ever went hunting…"